LEGENDS OF WARFARE

NAVAL

USS New York (BB-34)

From World War I to the Atomic Age

DAVID DOYLE

SCHIFFER MILITARY

4880 Lower Valley Road   Atglen, PA 19310

Designed by Justin Watkinson
Type set in Impact/Minion Pro/Univers LT Std

ISBN: 978-0-7643-5824-1
Printed in China

Published by Schiffer Publishing, Ltd.
4880 Lower Valley Road
Atglen, PA 19310
Phone: (610) 593-1777; Fax: (610) 593-2002
E-mail: Info@schifferbooks.com
www.schifferbooks.com

For our complete selection of fine books on this and related subjects, please visit our website at www.schifferbooks.com. You may also write for a free catalog.

Schiffer Publishing's titles are available at special discounts for bulk purchases for sales promotions or premiums. Special editions, including personalized covers, corporate imprints, and excerpts, can be created in large quantities for special needs. For more information, contact the publisher.

We are always looking for people to write books on new and related subjects. If you have an idea for a book, please contact us at proposals@schifferbooks.com.

Acknowledgments

While working on this book I was blessed with the generous help of Tom Kailbourn, Scott Taylor, Tracy White, Sean Hert, Roger Torgeson, Rick Davis, James Noblin, Dana Bell, and Dave Baker. As always, I could have done none of this without the support of my wonderful wife, Denise, who took notes, scanned photographs, and accompanied me on numerous research expeditions. She truly is a great blessing to me.

Contents

Introduction

Before the subject of this book, BB-34, was commissioned, there were four previous US Navy ships to bear the name USS *New York*. Shown here is the fourth such ship, the armored cruiser designated ACR-2. Commissioned in 1893, this cruiser saw combat in the Spanish-American War. Later, it was renamed USS *Saratoga* (1911) and USS *Rochester* (1917). *National Archives*

In the early years of the twentieth century, the battleship was the most powerful and fearsome weapon in a nation's arsenal. Termed "capital ships," a battleship could project one nation's power onto the shores of another nation or could form an offshore defensive perimeter for the nation whose flag was flown from its mast. These behemoths were truly technological marvels of their age, featuring massive yet precise elements, and these vessels came with a tremendous financial cost, not only in construction and fitting out, but also in crewing and upkeep. In the US Navy, with but one exception, battleships bore the names of states. Construction of a sophisticated and expensive warship is undertaken only with a great deal of advance planning. In an era well before that of any electronic computer, legions of engineers and draftsmen labored long hours. The age of the battleship predated so-called political correctness, and the massive vessels were typically referred to in the feminine form (she, her), and as with all US Navy vessels, the ships are considered almost a living entity—the US Navy style manual even states, "Do not use 'the' in front of a ship's name"— and certainly each battleship had its own personality and was held by the crew with a level of affection comparable to that of a person.

At the time of construction of Battleship 34, *New York*, began, it was customary to begin planning two years out in order to finalize the plans and secure the needed congressional appropriation for the construction and fitting out.

Notably, the official nomenclature at the time was, as above, "Battleship 34," but the growth of subtypes of smaller vessels led the Navy to develop a new classification system that was introduced on July 17, 1920; thereafter, the official nomenclature for battleships was changed to "BB"—thus *New York*, Battleship 34, became BB-34 *New York*.

Prior to the decision to name battleships—and battleships alone—after states, armored cruisers had been named for states. Thus, in order to avoid duplicate names, the decision to name Battleship 34 *New York* meant that the 1893-era armored cruiser *New York* had to be renamed. The name chosen was *Saratoga*, but that name too was later changed to *Rochester*, in order to free up the name *Saratoga* for use on Battlecruiser 3. However, owing to treaty limitations, Battlecruiser 3 was instead completed as an aircraft carrier.

CHAPTER 1
Construction

This large-scale, highly detailed model represents the fifth USN ship to bear the name *New York*. Designated BB-34, it would be constructed between 1911 and 1912 and would see service in two world wars. It would be the lead ship of the two-ship *New York* class of battleships, the other ship being its sister, USS *Texas* (BB-35). *Library of Congress*

In early 1909, as the Navy General Board began to consider Battleships 34 and 35, it contemplated the possibility of arming the vessels with 14-inch main guns, which at that time existed only on paper. To accommodate these weapons, the board turned to design 502, drawn in 1908, which featured five turrets, each housing two of the huge weapons.

The two new battleships were authorized by Congress on June 14, 1910. Whereas solicitation of construction bids for one of these two ships began on September 27, 1910, no bids were sought for the other. The lead ship of the new class, Battleship 34, *New York*, would be built by the New York Navy Yard, a government installation that was therefore not required to go through the bid process. Her sister, *Texas*, was to be built by the commercial shipyard the Newport News Shipbuilding and Drydock Company, as the result of competitive bidding. At the time, the two vessels designated Battleships 34 and 35 were to be the largest battleships in the world.

The keel of *New York* was laid on September 11, 1911, at Brooklyn Navy Yard, New York. This was five months after the keel of *Texas* was laid, but US Navy custom is that the class designation of its vessels be assigned on the basis of hull number—thus the ships were *New York* class, rather than *Texas*.

New York was to be powered by a pair of 14,050-horsepower vertical triple-expansion steam engines made by New York Engineering Company. These were fed by fourteen Babcock & Wilcox coal-fired boilers. Steam from the boilers would first enter a 39-inch-diameter high-pressure cylinder, be exhausted from there to a 63-inch-diameter intermediate-pressure cylinder, and then exhausted into a pair of 83-inch-diameter low-pressure cylinders. The stroke of pistons in each of these cylinders was 4 feet. The crankshafts of these engines would each drive an 18-foot, 7-inch-diameter, three-bladed propeller through their own 142-foot-long shaft. These engines, the largest of the type ever made, remained in use for the life of the ships, unlike many US Navy ships of the era, which were subsequently repowered.

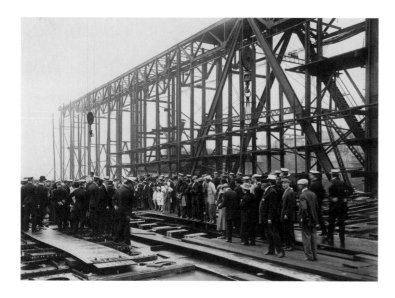

Although it took much work, planning, and fabricating to get to this point, the ceremonial start of construction of the battleship *New York* was the laying down of the keel on Monday, September 11, 1911, at the Navy Yard, New York, also known as the Brooklyn Navy Yard. In this traditional ceremony, dignitaries, naval officers, and shipyard officials and workers are gathered here to witness the first sections of the keel being lowered onto the building ways and the first rivets being driven. *National Archives*

After the keel-laying ceremony, some of the plates forming the bottom of the hull have been assembled on the building ways, sometimes called the building slip. The ship was built on the inclined ways with the stern nearest the water, and the view is from the area where the stern will take shape, facing forward. On tracks overhead are the big, cantilevered cranes that will deliver materials and machinery to the ship as it is constructed. *Library of Congress*

The beginnings of the keel and the bottom of the hull of *New York* are viewed from the forward end, facing toward Wallabout Basin, with the Manhattan tower of the Williamsburg Bridge faintly visible in the distance. Wooden shoring and cribbing were constructed on the ways to bear the weight of the hull plates and frame members. *National Archives*

This photo, apparently dating to September 11, 1911, was taken from a position closer to the hull in progress than in the preceding photo. At the center, plates are laid down that will form the bottom of the keel. In subsequent days and weeks, the keel will be built up to form the firm bottom frame of the hull. Lying to the side of the keel are steel plates that will form the bottom of the shell: the outer skin of the ship. *Library of Congress*

In a final photo from the day of the keel laying, September 11, 1911, yard workers go about the first stages of assembling the bottom of the hull, as seen from aft facing forward. In the foreground is some of the cribbing and shoring that will support the hull as work proceeds aft toward the stern. To the sides is staging, or scaffolding, that will come into play as construction of the hull advances. *National Archives*

In a November 20, 1911, view from the bow, in the foreground is the keel plate, on top of which were triangular brackets with lightening holes that braced the vertical keel: the long, upright member of the keel structure. The various steel plates have been predrilled for rivets and bolts. A bit farther aft is the forward point to which construction of the frames has reached. In the background, workmen have installed wooden timbers to brace the center of a lateral steel beam. *National Archives*

Almost ten weeks and one day after the keel laying, construction of the bottom and sides of the hull of the *New York* had advanced to this point, as documented in a photo taken on November 20, 1911. The double bottom of the hull is under construction, with some of the frames visible to the side and in the foreground where the inner-bottom plates have yet to be installed. In the foreground is a stove for heating rivets red hot. *National Archives*

The opposite end of the hull from that shown in the preceding photo is viewed facing forward on November 20, 1911. The keel in the area where the bottom of the hull begins to taper toward the stern is shown under construction in the foreground. The triangular brackets that brace the vertical keel are apparent. *National Archives*

Work on the hull of the *New York* has advanced in this photograph from December 18, 1911, and the cross sections of the frames are getting smaller as work approaches the stem of the bow. Wooden shores support the structure. Within the hull, workmen are erecting a longitudinal bulkhead, propped up with wooden braces. In the background, construction is well underway on a transverse bulkhead.
National Archives

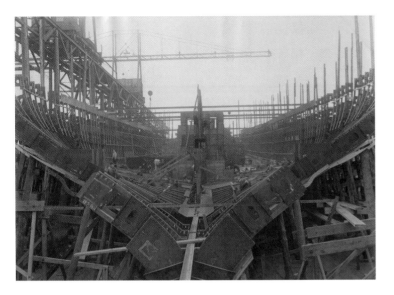

Another photograph from December 18, 1911, shows the hull of the *New York* from the point toward the stern to which construction of the frame has reached. The frames that formed the lateral ribs of the hull were numbered consecutively from the bow to the stern, 1 to 141. They were spaced 4 feet apart. *National Archives*

Taken farther aft from the perspective of the immediately preceding photo, on the port side of the hull facing forward in the hold on December 17, 1911, a series of transverse bulkheads are under construction. These would be parts of the enclosures for the boiler rooms. To the far right is bulkhead 78, which coincided with frame 78; the next bulkhead to the front is bulkhead 69. Together, these bulkheads would form the front and the rear of the aft of the three boiler rooms. *National Archives*

In a view of the forward part of the *New York* on December 17, 1911, running along the centerline is a longitudinal bulkhead that eventually will be two levels high, running from frames 18 to 41 both in the hold and the second platform. The area along the bulkhead will contain several magazines and storerooms and a compressor room. *National Archives*

Taken in the starboard side of the hold of the *New York*, looking aft on December 17, 1911, work is underway on the protective structure that will house the engine rooms. This structure was located between frames 89 and 104. *National Archives*

On January 22, 1912, a photographer took this view of the *New York* from one of the cantilever cranes, above the amidships area facing forward. In the foreground is transverse bulkhead number 69, which was in line with frame 69. Immediately forward of that bulkhead is the middle boiler room. *National Archives*

The port bow of the *New York* is seen in this photograph from February 29, 1912, showing some of the cribbing and shoring that supported this part of the hull well above ground level. There was enough room under the bow to allow a shipyard railroad to pass underneath it. *National Archives*

Another photo taken from a cantilever crane on January 22, 1912, overlooks the machinery spaces facing aft. In the background can be seen partially completed frames in the area forward of the stern. Just the keel of the stern forward of where the rudder will be mounted has been started, with the bend in that part of the keel faintly visible in the distance. *National Archives*

By February 29, 1912, the frame of the stern of the *New York* was beginning to take shape, as seen from aft and starboard. Although it is hard to see because of the shadows and the scaffolding, the bottom of the stern is lower than the planks in the foreground. The bottom part of the stern as seen here would contain trimming tanks, while the upper part would contain the steering room and the steering gear. *National Archives*

A few days later, on March 2, 1912, a photographer used a cantilever crane as a vantage point for taking this photo looking forward over a maze of bulkheads, beams, and frame members. The hull was slowly rising in height, a deck or a platform at a time, but it still had more levels to go before the main deck was laid down, near the level of the tops of the scaffolding posts. *National Archives*

On March 21, 1912, the port strut, to support the port propeller shaft, is being maneuvered into position for installation. The upper part of the stern, as far as it had been constructed by that date, is topped with an armored platform with sloping sides to protect the steering room and steering gear. *National Archives*

Another view dated March 2, 1912, shows the progress of construction of the *New York,* facing aft. In the foreground are vertical frame sections. These were fabricated a level at a time and were clad with inner and outer hull plating, creating voids between the two shells. In between the shells, compartments are being constructed. *National Archives*

The framed and partially plated platform over the steering room and steering gear, seen from the port side in the preceding photo, is viewed from above in this April 1, 1912, view facing forward from off the port stern. On the starboard side of the hull in the foreground, plates for the inner shell of the hull have been assembled; a number of manholes are visible on the shell. *National Archives*

The highest level of the construction of the bulkheads and transverse beams at the time this photograph was taken on April 1, 1912, was the third deck. In the foreground, compartments are still under construction on the first platform, one level below the third deck. At the exact center of the photo is transverse bulkhead number 26 with a door in it, which formed the forward bulkhead of the 14-inch ammunition handling room for turret 1. *National Archives*

As seen from off the port bow on May 11, 1912, the third deck is only partially framed in the forward area of the hull. In the foreground, the inner and outer shell plates and the frames between them are visible. At the extreme left is frame 10. The spaces between the inner and outer plates formed chambers that in some cases served as voids and in others as oil reservoirs. *National Archives*

By May 11, 1912, the installation of STS (special treatment steel) armor decking was well underway on the third deck, as viewed from over the steering-gear compartment near the stern, facing forward. It was from the third deck upward that the barbettes, the heavily armored foundations for the five turrets, would be constructed. Amidships are numerous openings in the deck for the uptakes. *National Archives*

In a photograph from May 11, 1912, construction on the stern above the steering-gear compartment has begun, for which purpose scaffolding has been erected. To the far right, the curved frame for the stern is in place. Faintly visible in the shadows at the center of the photo is the port propeller strut. *National Archives*

There were two engine rooms in the *New York*, a port one and a starboard one, side by side. One of them is shown in a June 9, 1912, photo after the engine foundations had been installed but before the engines were installed. The ship was to be powered by two dual-acting (i.e., single-stroke), triple-expansion, reciprocating steam engines, rated at 28,100 horsepower. The engines were to be powered by steam from fourteen Babcock and Wilcox coal-fired boilers with oil-spray boosters, for rapid increases in boiler temperatures when required. *National Archives*

As seen from the stern on June 9, 1912, the armored platform with the sloping sides over the steering-gear compartment and steering room is completed. In the background, the beams to support the second deck are under construction. Poking up through those beams is the barbette of turret 5, also under construction. *National Archives*

A June 9, 1912, view facing aft on the third deck to the port side of where the barbette of turret 2 soon will be built; to the far left is the forward bulkhead of the forward dynamo-room trunk, at frame 42½. Just aft of the trunk is the location where central station will be constructed. In the background, the barbettes for turrets 3 and 4 are under construction. *National Archives*

The barbette of turret 1 stands above the third deck in this June 9, 1912, view facing toward the bow from frame 45. To the rear of the barbette and next to the sawhorse is a round opening in the deck, with a ladder protruding through it. This opening is centered where the barbette of turret 2 will be constructed. *National Archives*

A forest of scaffolding posts and planks enclose the aft half of the hull of the *New York* in a photo from off the starboard side on July 2, 1912. Below and forward of the cantilever crane, the barbette for turret 4 is faintly visible above the shell of the hull. Shell plating is gradually being installed on the sides of the stern. *National Archives*

The *New York* is viewed from the port side amidships facing forward on July 2, 1912, with barbettes 1 and 2 in the background. The closest lateral beam coincides with frame 65. Rough timbers are used to brace the beams. Below the beams are openings for uptake trunks. *National Archives*

In a photograph that is an exact continuation of the right side of the preceding photo, the forward half of the hull of the *New York* is seen from the starboard side on July 2, 1912. Barbette 2, which had not been begun when the June 9 photographs were taken, now stands taller than barbette 1 to its front. In the foreground are stocks of building materials, from timbers to shell plates, framing members, and other fittings. *National Archives*

In another view from the port side of the *New York* on July 2, 1912, *from left to right*, barbettes 3, 4, and 5 are visible in succession, facing aft. The barbettes were constructed of class A armor, with a maximum thickness of 12 inches, tapering down to as little as 4 inches at the bases of the barbettes on the third deck. *National Archives*

The bow of the *New York* was photographed from a building at the Navy Yard, New York, around early July 1912. Visible through the scaffolding at the bottom of the photo is the ship's bulbous bow, a feature designed to reduce drag and enhance stability, speed, range, and fuel efficiency. *Library of Congress*

As seen from the stern on the second deck, also known at that time as the gun deck, all the barbettes except number 1 are visible in an August 13, 1912, photo. In this view and preceding ones, it is noticeable how the frames of the ship tapered the higher the deck, so that by the time they reached the second deck they were quite small in section. *National Archives*

The photographer stood on the forecastle of the main deck on August 13, 1912, to take this view of the *New York*. At this time, the forecastle was the highest section of deck that had been framed, extending back to the beam at frame 16 in the foreground. Beyond are the incomplete barbettes, the nearest two being numbers 1 and 2. With two and a half months remaining until launching, much work remained to be done. *National Archives*

The photographer stood on the port side of the second deck on August 13, 1912, to take this view of the half deck, one level below. The rear of the half deck terminated at an angle from each side of barbette 2. Below the angled rear of the half deck, several workmen are visible on the third deck. To the right is the dynamo-room trunk, to which was attached on each side a trunk for a 3-inch ammunition hoist. *National Archives*

By September 17, 1912, when this view from amidships was taken facing aft, most of the main deck had been framed and plated. In the foreground, two ovoid openings have been cut in the main deck; the removed plate to the right is marked "Don't Cut Beam." Aft of the second opening, a mooring bitt rests on the deck prior to installation. *National Archives*

With only two weeks left before the launching of the *New York*, its rudder is being hoisted into position for setting it on its mountings on October 15, 1912. Light-colored primer has been daubed on many of the fasteners on the rudder, and someone has painted a head on the lower part of it, although it is hard to tell if looks like a moose or elk. *National Archives*

In another photo taken on September 17, 1912, from the port side of the second deck aft of barbette 2, a diagonal armor bulkhead has been constructed one level below, at the rear of the half deck. Wooden shoring temporarily supports the bulkhead. In the foreground is a trunk for a 5-inch ammunition hoist. Barbette 3, still under construction, is hidden in the shadows under the main deck in the background. *National Archives*

The mountings are ready for setting the rudder on the *New York*, on October 15, 1912. Large pins will secure the gudgeons, or sockets, at the rear of the rudder to the gudgeons mounted on the hull. Above the upper gudgeon on the hull in this photo is the bottom of the rudder stock, which translated mechanical force from the steering gear to the rudder. Each side of the tiller was perforated with six holes, to accept large bolts to secure the rudder stock to the top of the rudder. Draft marks are painted on the hull; next to them, and also on the aft propeller shaft strut to the left, are zinc plates, which acted as galvanic anodes to protect the steel surfaces from corrosion. *National Archives*

Shortly after the preceding photo was taken, workmen help guide the rudder onto its mountings. The rudder is cradled in a sling made of steel cables, attached to the hoist cable. A chain hoist attached to a clevis on the hull is being used to maneuver the rudder gudgeons into place. *National Archives*

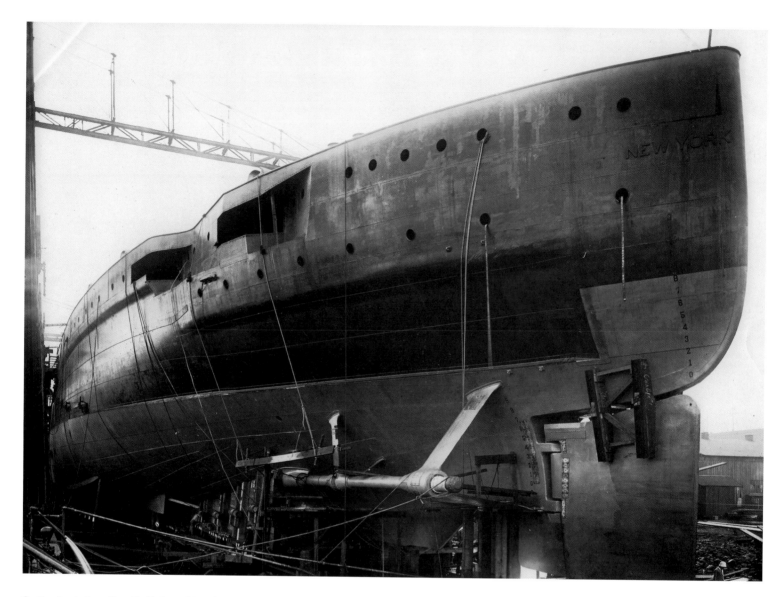

On the day before *New York*'s launching, October 29, 1912, the hull is viewed from off the port stern. Each propeller shaft housing was supported by two V-shaped strut assemblies. Other details worthy of notice include the ship's name in raised letters on the stern; the casemates on the second deck, where 5-inch guns will be mounted; the lock on the rudder to immobilize it during launching; and the two portside bilge keels, the finlike structures on the bottom of the hull in the background. *National Archives*

In the days and weeks before its launching, the *New York*'s hull, by then weighing 9,700 tons, had been methodically transferred from the cribbing, shores, and blocks it was constructed on, to the launching ways, on which the hull would slide into the water. As seen in a photo taken on October 28, 1912, wooden cribbing has been installed forward of the propeller shaft. Timber shores had been snugged under the hull inboard of the bilge keels. *National Archives*

CHAPTER 2
Launching, Fitting Out, and Commissioning

For thirteen months the hull of *New York* rose steadily over the builder's ways of the Brooklyn Navy Yard until finally, in October 1912, the hull was sufficiently completed that it could be launched. While capable of floating, at this stage the ship was far from complete.

The launching of a capital ship, especially during this era, was a very prestigious affair. For the October 30, 1912, launching, in addition to the ship's sponsor, Elsie Calder, the daughter of William Calder, US Representative from New York, the launching was attended by a wide array of dignitaries. This in part could have had something to do with the timing, since the launch date was one week before the presidential election.

In addition to Miss Calder and 500 shipyard workers directly involved in the launch process, there were 40,000 other visitors present, including President William Howard Taft, Secretary of the Navy George von Lengerke Meyer, Governor John A. Dix, and New York mayor William J. Gaynor.

Counter to what many think, when a ship is launched, especially a ship of any size, the construction process is far from over. Many months of labor by a legion of workers remain to be done before the vessel can put to sea. At launch the ship was little more than an empty shell; the fitting-out period equipped the vessel with weapons, machinery, stoves, steering gear, lighting, and the myriad of other items needed on a ship at sea, and at war.

Finally, on April 15, 1914, *New York* was ready to join the US fleet—to become a commissioned US Navy warship.

The launching of any US Navy capital ship was the occasion of a gathering of naval and civilian dignitaries. The launching of the *New York* on October 30, 1912, drew its share, including President William Howard Taft, at the center with his right hand hiding his face. *Library of Congress*

Its bow decorated with bunting, the *New York* is prepared for its christening and launching. On the stand next to the bow is the sponsor's party and dignitaries, including President Taft and Secretary of the Navy George Meyer. In preparation for the moment of launching, workmen had spent the preceding hours methodically removing shoring, cribbing, and keel blocks from underneath the hull; driving wedges to transfer the weight of the hull; and performing other preparatory procedures. *National Archives*

A moment after the preceding photo was taken, the ship's sponsor, Miss Elsie Calder, the daughter of Congressman William M. Calder of Brooklyn, prepares to break the ceremonial bottle of champagne on the bow to christen the *New York*. Immediately afterward, two hydraulic triggers, one on each side of the launching slip, would be actuated, releasing the sliding ways the hull rested on, allowing it to slide down the greased launching ways. *National Archives*

USS *New York* General Data, 1914

Dimensions

Length overall	573′ ¾″
Waterline length	565′ 7¼″
Maximum beam	95′ 2⅝″
Normal draft	28′ 5⅜″
Deep draft	29′ 8¼″
Builder	New York Navy Yard
Laid Down	September 11, 1911
Launched	October 30, 1912
Commissioned	April 15, 1914

Displacement Standard	27,000 tons
Displacement Full Load	28,367 tons

Armor Protection

Total Armor Weight	8,368.3 tons
Belt	From frame 18 to 122, 12″ thick top tapering to 10″ thick at bottom. From frame 122 to 137, 6″ thick. Height is 7′ 11½″ throughout.
Ends	Forward at frame 18: 10″ thick at centerline and 11″ thick outboard. Height is 7′ 11½″ throughout.
Aft From Frame 137	9″ from top of stern post to second deck
Decks	100 lb. STS + 20 lb. aft; 60 lb. STS + 20 lb. amidships; 40 lb. STS + 20 lb. forward of belt
Turrets	Face plates: 14″; Sides: 8″ increased to 9″ near front; Rear: 8″; Top: 4″
Barbettes	12″ above second deck, 5″ between second and half decks
Conning Tower	12″ sides, 8″ on top

Machinery

Total Weight	2,390 tons (with liquids)
Boilers	Fourteen Babcock & Wilcox (8 superheated); 65,480 ft.² total heating surface
Engines	Two vertical, four-cylinder, triple-expansion engines: one right-hand rotation, one left-hand rotation.
Each Engine	High-pressure cylinder, 41″ diameter; Intermediate cylinder, 62″ diameter; Two low-pressure cylinders, 82″ diameter each. Stroke of 48″.
Shaft Horsepower	28,100 maximum ahead
Maximum Speed	21.0 knots

Endurance

10 Knots	7,060 nautical miles
Generators	Four 300 kw, 125-volt DC turbogenerator sets
Propellers	Two three-bladed, 18′ 7¾″ diameter
Rudders	One, balanced
Fuel	1,900 tons coal, 400 tons oil
Complement	1,052 total (58 officers; 944 enlisted)

As the assembled crowd cheers it on, the *New York* has almost reached the bottom of the launching slip. Under its bow is the fore poppet, a type of cribbing temporarily attached to the hull to stabilize the hull on its downward slide. Towering above the hull is a cantilever crane. *Library of Congress*

The *New York* is fully afloat upon launching on October 30, 1912. A number of official personnel were on the ship during the launching to perform a number of tasks, such as measuring the speed of the hull as it slid down the ways, taking soundings, observing any unusual flexing or distortion of the ship, noting any leaks that appeared, and pumping out any water that entered the hull. *National Archives*

As seen from its port side, the impetus of its launching carries the *New York* stern-first out into Wallabout Basin at the Navy Yard, New York. For the occasion, the hull was dressed from stem to stern with flags and pennants. Tugboats in the foreground stand by to assist the ship to its fitting-out dock, once it has ceased moving. *National Archives*

The torpedo-tube ports on the starboard side of the *New York* are visible in this view of tugboats nudging the hull toward the fitting-out dock on launching day, October 30, 1912. The only significant structures above the main deck at this point were the barbettes, the beginnings of the superstructure, and several temporary huts. *National Archives*

The tugboats move out toward the *New York*. The ship was drawing water well below its established waterline. In the light-colored area below the waterline are two staggered openings for torpedo tubes, part of the ship's defenses, as built. *National Archives*

By the time this photo was taken on May Day 1913, the *New York* had been undergoing postlaunching construction at a fitting-out dock at the Navy Yard, New York, for six months. Work had advanced on the superstructure, and scaffolding was rigged along the side of the hull. Wooden planking covered the area above and below the designed waterline, where the belt armor will be applied later. This planking, which starts just forward of and below the forward casemate, also is seen in some of the photos of the launching. *National Archives*

A May 1, 1913, photo taken on the starboard side of the main deck shows the rear of the first level of the superstructure in the foreground. This part of the superstructure will house the crew's galley. In the background to the right is the king post of the starboard boat crane. The front of the superstructure has attained several levels. *National Archives*

In a photo taken on the main deck at the stern on May 1, 1913, in the foreground, just forward of the temporary boom and the hatch, is the opening for barbette 5, forward of which is the taller barbette 4. In the distance are the superstructure and the king post of the starboard boat crane. *National Archives*

Turret 2 for the *New York* is being lifted from blocks on the fitting-out pier at the Navy Yard, New York, and is about to be hoisted into place on barbette 2. The number "2" is painted in several places on the gunhouse and the gun pit, the tub under the gunhouse. The 14-inch/45-caliber guns and the roof and frontal plate of the turret eventually will be installed after the turret is landed, or seated on the barbette. *National Archives*

After turret 2 was lifted from the fitting-out pier, it was placed on a yard craft called the *Hercules* and brought alongside the *New York*. Here, one of the big cranes at the Navy Yard, New York, has just lifted the turret from the *Hercules* and is bringing it to the *New York* on May 8, 1913. *National Archives*

Turret 2 has been landed on its barbette, and workers make ready to release the gigantic crane hook from the turret. The steel sides of the turret at this point in time were composed of relatively thin backing plates. Later, the sides would be built up over the backing plates so that they were between 8-inch- and 9-inch-thick class A (face-hardened) armor. *National Archives*

Turret 2 is ready for landing on its barbette on the *New York* on May 8, 1913. The view is from the front of barbette 1, and turret 2 is oriented with its front toward the camera. The trunnion mounts for the 14-inch/45-caliber guns are visible in the front of the turret. *National Archives*

A 14-inch/45-caliber gun is being hoisted to its mount in turret 2 on May 22, 1913. The barrel just forward of the breech fitted through a large casting called the sleeve. The sleeve included a trunnion on each side, on which the gun pivoted in elevation. The sleeve also served as a slide for the gun to recoil and recuperate in. Below the sleeve were recoil and counterrecoil cylinders, the pistons of which were connected to the large lug on the bottom of the breech. A sign on the muzzle end of the gun reads "DANIELS." *National Archives*

A crane boat called the *Capitol* delivers the aft smokestack to the *New York* on July 2, 1913. The forward smokestack already is installed. By this time, much of the belt armor had been installed on the hull, providing extra protection above and below the waterline. The level of the superstructure had not risen since the time the May 1, 1913, photographs were taken. *National Archives*

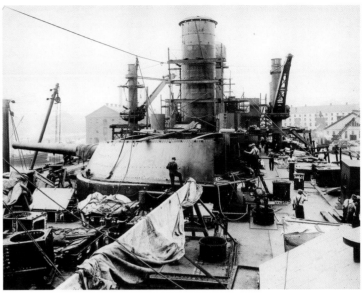

Both guns had been mounted in turret 3 when this photo was taken on July 9, 1913. The view is facing forward, with the smokestacks, the rear of the superstructure, and the two boat cranes appearing in the background. The backing plates were on turret 3, and several roof beams are visible, but the rear of the turret was open. *National Archives*

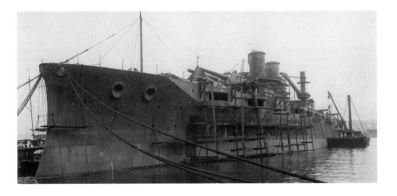

The *New York* is seen from the port side in a July 9, 1913, general view. The wooden planks on the hull that are visible in the photos of the ship's launching and in the May 1, 1913, photo of the ship were covered over with belt armor. Workers refurbishing the *New York*'s sister ship, the *Texas*, almost eighty years after it was built encountered wooden planking behind the belt armor and reported that the wood was still in excellent condition. *National Archives*

Weapons and Ballistics

Weapon	Ammo Type	Gun Model	Projectile Mark	Projectile Weight	Explosive Charge	Muzzle Velocity	Range Yards
14″/45 cal.	Armor Piercing	3	20	1,400 lbs.	31.5 lbs.	2,600 fps	21,000
14″/45 cal.	Armor Piercing	8	20	1,500 lbs.	22.9 lbs.	2,600 fps	23,000
14″/45 cal.	High Capacity	8	19	1,275 lbs.	104.2 lbs.	2,735 fps	23,500
5″/51 cal.	Common	13	15	50 lbs.	4.3 lbs.	3,150 fps	17,100
5″/51 cal.	High Capacity	13	39	50 lbs.	26.4 lbs.	3,150 fps	17,100
3″/50 cal.	APCBC	21	29	13.1 lbs.	1.2 lbs.	2,700 fps	29,800
3″/50 cal.	High Capacity	21	27	13.1 lbs.	5.7 lbs.	2,700 fps	29,800
3″/50 cal.	AAC	21	27	13.1 lbs.	5.7 lbs.	2,700 fps	29,800

With six months yet to go until commissioning, fitting-out work continues on the *New York* at the Navy Yard, New York, on October 4, 1913. Turrets 1 and 2 have received their side armor and roofs, and turret 2 has its frontal plate of 14-inch class A armor. The conning tower, the heavily armored navigating and fire control center of the ship during battle, is substantially completed to the rear of turret 2; vision slits are visible near the top of the tower. Aft of the smokestacks, construction is well underway on the cage-type mainmast. *National Archives*

The *New York* is viewed off its port stern in an October 5, 1913, photograph. The gunhouses of turrets 4 and 5 are not completed, and they are covered with tarpaulins. Covers, some with portholes, have been installed on the casemates. In the stern is a port for a 5-inch/51-caliber gun. This gun position would prove to be a mistake and eventually would be eliminated and the port covered over. *National Archives*

The port side of the *New York* from the bow to amidships is displayed in the fitting-out dock at the Navy Yard, New York, on October 5, 1913. The port boat crane, encased in scaffolding, is toward the right. A large ventilator is to the side of the forward smokestack. Turrets 1 and 2 are traversed to starboard. *National Archives*

The *New York* is observed from the mainmast to the stern in a photograph from October 5, 1913. On the deck between turrets 3 and 4 are large ventilators. The cage-type mainmast was constructed of crisscrossing, diagonal pipes, clamped together at their intersections and reinforced by several horizontal rings. *National Archives*

Construction of the battleship *New York* approaches completion around January 1914. The foremast is now present, and the fighting tops on the tops of the masts, which will house spotting and fire control stations, are under construction with scaffolding around their lower levels. Partway up the foremast is a platform on which two covered searchlights are mounted. *National Archives*

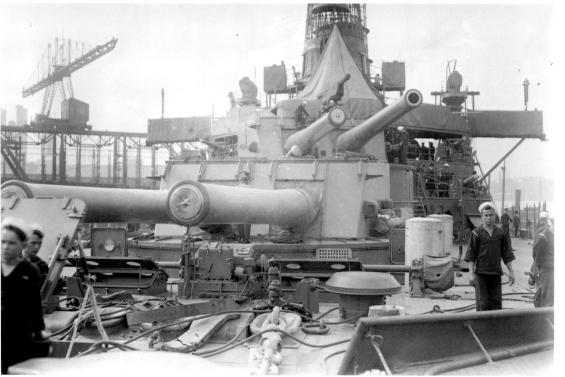

Many details are apparent in this view from the forecastle of the *New York* around the time of its commissioning. In the foreground are the three anchor-chain pipes leading to the chain lockers below decks. Farther aft are hatches and turrets 1 and 2. Canvas windscreens have been lashed to the railings of the bridges; the windscreens on the searchlight platform hide the searchlights from view. Contrasting against a tipi-shaped cover atop the conning tower is a rangefinder with a cover over it on top of turret 2. *Library of Congress*

One of the twenty-one 5-inch/51-caliber gun mounts on the *New York* as built is viewed from the upper rear. This piece was at the forward end of the starboard side of the superstructure deck, one level above the main deck. The maker's mark on the top of the breech identifies the gun as a 5-inch Mk. VII, number 448, manufactured by the Midvale Steel Company of Philadelphia, Pennsylvania. *Library of Congress*

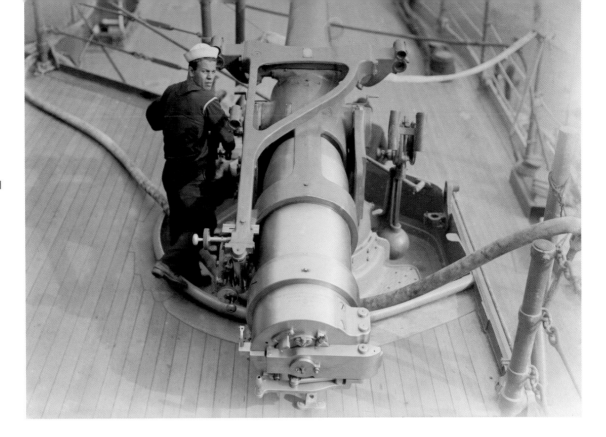

Turrets 1 and 2 are viewed from the forward starboard corner of the superstructure deck in early 1914. Under cover in the foreground is the same 5-inch/51-caliber gun mount seen in the preceding photo. On the forecastle is a large wooden frame of a type often seen on photos of battleships being fitted out during this era. The frame seems to have been used in aligning the main-battery guns. *Library of Congress*

Fourteen-inch shells for the battleship *New York*'s primary battery are on the quarterdeck prior to being lowered to the magazines far below decks. To the right is the rear of one of the ship's motorboats in its storage cradle. *Library of Congress*

The original inscription on this photograph is "Jackies on 14″ gun—'New York.'" Jackies was period slang for US Navy sailors. Several crewmen are leaning on a box-shaped unit with open doors and a grille: this was a ventilator from which the air scoop has been removed and is lying on the deck in the foreground. *Library of Congress*

US battleships of the pre–World War II period typically carried onboard a variety of utility boats, from motor launches and motor whaleboats up to the barges used by the ship's commander or admiral. Here, a crane is hoisting one of the *New York*'s motor launches, on which the propeller and propeller shaft are not installed. *Library of Congress*

Blue jackets getting deck lashings in shape prior to the commissioning ceremony. *Library of Congress*

On the morning of April 15, 1914, the officers and crew of the battleship *New York* are assembled on the quarterdeck during the commissioning ceremony, in which the ship is formally transferred to its first commanding officer, in this case Capt. Thomas Slidell Rodgers, and is placed in active service in the US Navy. Here, the ensign is being raised on the flagstaff on the stern.

The ensign flies from the flagstaff of the *New York* at 1033 on April 15, 1914, during the commissioning ceremony. With the commissioning, the ship assumed the title of "USS," or United States Ship, a title it would bear until decommissioned at the end of its active career. *National Archives*

CHAPTER 3
To War

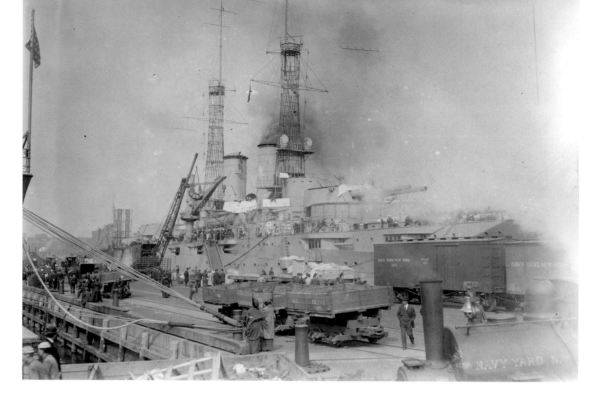

USS *New York* is docked at the Navy Yard, New York, and is taking on crewmen and supplies on April 24, 1914. On the roof of turret 2 is the tripod stand and holder for an optical rangefinder, on which the rangefinder is not installed. Smoke is issuing from the forward smokestack, indicating that some of the coal-burning forward boilers have been lit. *Library of Congress*

The commissioning was followed by a shakedown cruise in the Caribbean, and then *New York* was dispatched to Veracruz, pursuant to President Woodrow Wilson's ordering Rear Admiral Frank Friday Fletcher to put an amphibious force ashore at Veracruz in response to the "Mexican Incident."

Mexico had been in the throes of a revolution since 1911, and US citizens, a substantial number of whom worked in the oil industry in Tampico, adjacent to Veracruz, were increasingly at risk as rival Mexican factions battled each other. On April 9, 1914, crewmen of a US gunboat were detained by Mexican forces in Tampico, in an incident that escalated and led to Wilson's order to land troops in Veracruz. On April 21, 502 Marines and 285 armed sailors deployed at Veracruz, with the aim of seizing the customs house to intercept an expected arms delivery. Met with resistance, Fletcher requested additional reinforcements. Those reinforcements included new sister ships *Texas* and *New York*, the latter of which would become Fletcher's flagship.

A tradition was begun aboard *New York* in December 1915, which soon spread through the US fleet. Moored at Brooklyn Navy Yard, the officers and men of the battleship suggested to their captain, Capt. (later Admiral) Hugh Rodman, that the ship give a Christmas party to as many orphans as the massive ship could accommodate. Rodman supported this, and as a result, for some time *New York* became known as the "Christmas ship."

On November 13, 1917, *New York*, flying the flag of then Admiral Hugh Rodman, commander of Battleship Division 9, stood out from Lynnhaven Roads, Virginia, for "distant service" with the British Grand Fleet at Scapa Flow. What should have become an easy voyage became near disastrous when Division 9 encountered severe weather, with sleet, hail, snow, and high winds. Capt. Henry Wiley of battleship *Wyoming* would later recall of that storm, "At the height of the gale, it blew as hard as I have ever seen it, and the seas were the worst I could recollect." Winds estimated at 100 miles per hour carried away the radio masts of all four battleships, and 250 tons of seawater entered the forward compartments of *New York*, pushing its bow down to the point that there was a risk of foundering. Three days of pumping and bailing relieved the situation.

Upon arrival at Scapa Flow, Battleship Division 9 became known as the 6th Battle Squadron of the Grand Fleet. It was during this service with the Grand Fleet that in February 1918, while in another gale, a *New York* crewman was lost when he was swept overboard.

In May 1918, *New York* was visited by Scotland's Duke and Duchess of Atholl.

On the evening of October 14, 1918, while leading a force escorting minelayers back into Pentland Firth, *New York* was rocked by the force of an underwater collision on its starboard side. This was followed almost immediately by a second underwater

This photo of the *New York* from the starboard side was taken on April 24, 1914, probably within moments of the preceding photo. Canvas covers fitted over the 14-inch guns and gunports of turret 2 are pulled back; these were much-simpler and more-compact affairs than the later bloomers used on the turrets. Note the lowered covers on the forward starboard casemate to the right of the photo. *Library of Congress*

A photo dated April 25, 1914, shows USS *New York* ten days after its commissioning. The ship has moved away from the pier, and what appears to be a coal barge is alongside it. A series of booms have been rigged along the main deck amidships for the purpose of hoisting aboard the supplies. *National Archives*

collision at the stern, which broke off two propeller blades, reducing the ship to one engine and a speed of 12 knots.

With the waters too deep for the underwater object to be a shoal or a shipwreck, the men aboard, including Admirals Rodman and Beatty, determined that *New York* must have collided with a submerged German U-boat, which first hit the side of the battleship and then was run down by the propeller. The collision certainly sank the submarine, later determined to have been the UB-113 or UB-123, resulting in the only sinking of a German vessel by Battleship Division 9.

Crippled, *New York*, under heavy escort, limped to Rosyth for repair. While en route, at 0100 on October 16, another U-boat launched three torpedoes at the battleship; fortunately, none found their mark.

During November a number of dignitaries visited the ship, starting with the November 3 visit of Crown Prince and Admiral Hirohito (later emperor) of Japan, followed seventeen days later by Britain's King George V and His Royal Highness the Prince of Wales. This was George V's second visit aboard, having been preceded on July 22 while being accompanied by the king and queen of Belgium.

Following the surrender of the German High Seas Fleet at Scapa Flow on November 21, 1918, *New York* reversed its course across the Atlantic and operated in the Caribbean until mid-1919, before being sent to the West Coast as part of the new Pacific Fleet.

The forward part of USS *New York*'s main deck is viewed from the searchlight platform at the Navy Yard, New York, on April 25, 1914. A rare view is available of the roofs of turrets 1 and 2 at this time. At the center of turret 2's roof is the tripod and mounting bracket for a rangefinder. On the main deck to the front of turret 1 are the three wildcats: the capstan heads of the windlasses that were geared to engage the anchor chains in order to raise and lower the anchors. Very soon the *New York* would depart for blockade duty off Veracruz, Mexico, deferring its builder's trials until later that year. *National Archives*

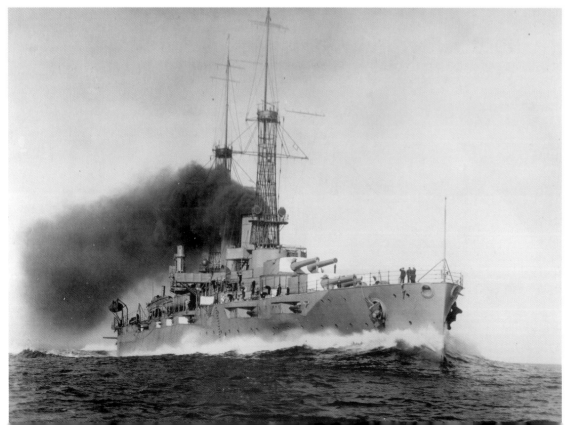

After its service off Veracruz, in September 1914 the USS *New York* was ordered back to the East Coast for its belated builder's trials. In one of a series of photos taken by Enrique Muller during these trials, the *New York* slices through the waves off Rockland, Maine, on a blustery day in late October 1914 (some sources have misdated this photo as May 29, 1915). The builder's trials were intended to disclose any mechanical problems or breakdowns so they could be remedied. Several of the 5-inch/51-caliber guns are traversed outward for drill or a firing exercise. Jutting out far to the side, one level below the navigating bridge, is the starboard wing bridge, with a canvas windscreen lashed to the railing. *National Archives*

The battleship *New York* cruises along the Maine coast during the October 1914 builder's trials. The white objects directly to the fronts of the muzzles of the guns of turret 1 and in the area between the barbettes of turrets 1 and 2 are windscreens for hatches. During speed runs conducted during the builder's trials, the ship achieved a maximum speed of 22.3 knots and an average of 21.6 knots, both of which exceeded sister ship *Texas*'s performance during its builder's trials. *Library of Congress*

By January 15, 1915, the *New York* had returned to the Navy Yard, New York, where it is shown docked. The *New York* would spend the next two years patrolling and training in the Atlantic. The foretop, the fire control tub on top of the cage part of the foremast, by now had a new shape, with a sharp angle running around the circumference of the horizontal centerline. *Library of Congress*

If the original inscriptions on the photographs are accurate, this photograph shows USS *New York* lying off its namesake city on January 16, 1915, the day after the preceding photo was taken. A noticeable difference in this photo is the dark-colored stripes now painted on the upper part of the aft smokestack. *National Archives*

In another photograph dated January 16, 1915, the *New York* is viewed off its port stern in New York Harbor. In these January 1915 photos, the turrets had sheets stretching completely across the frontal plates, with openings and flaps for the 14-inch guns. Also worthy of notice are the ventilator on the quarterdeck, the rangefinder with a cover mounted on a tripod atop turret 4; and the searchlight platform on the mainmast. *National Archives*

A helmsman is at his station on the navigating bridge of USS *New York* around early 1915. The bridge was completely open to the elements, so the helmsman is wearing a rain slicker and rubber boots. In addition to the helm, or steering wheel, the bridge included a binnacle; an engine-order telegraph, for signaling the engine room the desired engine direction and speed; and other controls and indicators. To the right is the front of the foremast, and to the front of the bridge is the roof of the conning tower. *Library of Congress*

During its pre–World War I cruises, USS *New York* occasionally visited the Port of Boston. On the occasion of this photograph, May 23, 1916, the battleship (*center*) was moored at the Navy Yard, Charleston, across the Charles River from Boston. At the time, it was serving as the flagship of Adm. DeWitt Coffman. Flanking it are USS *New Jersey* (BB-16), which was Adm. Coffman's second flagship (*left*), and USS *Virginia* (BB-13), Coffman's first flagship (*right*).

USS *New York* is anchored at Hampton Roads, Virginia, on December 10, 1916. A close examination of the photograph reveals that the fire control station on the mainmast now had an angled ring around it, possibly a wind deflector, and the fire control stations on both masts now had raised covers. *National Archives*

The battleship *New York* is viewed from the starboard side anchored at Hampton Roads on December 10, 1916. On the aft smokestack is a large, red letter *E*, indicating that the ship's engineering department had won that year's award for excellence. Note the light-colored covers on the casemates. The shapes faintly visible on top of the 14-inch guns near the fronts of the gunhouses are subcaliber guns with covers on them; these guns replicated the ballistic properties of the 14-inch guns and sometimes were used for firing practice to save on the cost of 14-inch shells and powder. *National Archives*

In 1915, the crew of the *New York* organized a Christmas party for hundreds of New York City orphans. This event would become a tradition in the US Navy. Here, children and their attendants file along the main deck of the *New York*, with Santa Claus at the left to greet them, at the Navy Yard, New York, in 1916. A big Christmas tree is on top of turret 2, and smaller ones are on top of the boat crane and other places. Two of the wildcats are seen close-up. *Maritime Quest*

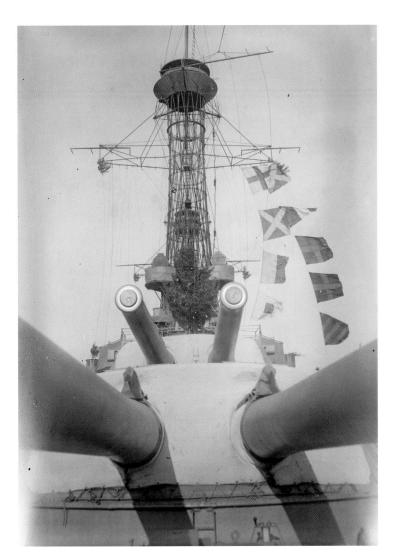

A photo from the front of turret 1 on December 25, 1916, reveals details of the lashings for the sheets covering the fronts of the turrets. Also in view are the various yardarms and radio antennas on the foremast; since the ship first went into service, more arms and antennas had been added to the yardarms, between the searchlight platform and the fighting top. At this time, the *New York*'s sister ship, the *Texas*, had two searchlight platforms, one immediately above the other. *Library of Congress*

The commander of USS *New York*, Capt. Charles F. Hughes, hands a large package to a boy, while Santa Claus holds a little girl during the Christmas party, on December 25, 1916. The Christmas party was the idea of the crew of the *New York*, and it demonstrated their bigheartedness and community spirit. *Library of Congress*

The *New York* was part of Battle Division 9, operating with the British Grand Fleet as the 6th Battle Squadron, during World War I. Following the end of the war, that squadron is seen anchored off Brest, France, on December 13, 1918, during President Woodrow Wilson's arrival at that port aboard USS *George Washington* (SP-3018), to the right.

In a view taken from the top of turret 2 facing aft at the Navy Yard, New York, on January 21, 1919, immediately aft of the turret is the conning tower. The vision slits in the tower had covers; the front one and one on the starboard side are open and are dangling from chain-type linkages. On the top front of the conning tower is an insulator for an antenna wire. Canvas curtains and top with windows had been installed over the navigating bridge. Above the bridge, the torpedo-defense platform had been expanded, now featuring a wind-deflector bulwark made of riveted sheet steel. *National Archives*

The *New York* is anchored off Rockaway, Long Island, on April 23, 1919. The round object on the front of the searchlight platform on the foremast is a range clock, also known as a concentration dial. This dial was used as a visual signal to neighboring ships in the battle line of the range to a designated target, to allow the other ships to quickly establish a range in the smoke of battle. *National Archives*

The navigating bridge of USS *New York* with the canvas curtains and top installed is seen at the Navy Yard, New York, on January 21, 1919. The helm has been removed from its stand. The clocklike instrument on the second stand from the left was the rudder indicator. Other features included a gyro repeater, course indicator, a standard compass, and an electric stand. *National Archives*

USS *New York* is viewed off its starboard stern off Rockaway, Long Island, on April 23, 1919. A close examination of the photo shows that by early 1919, the covers of the fighting tops, previously supported by a few light vertical frames, now were supported by more thicker frames. *National Archives*

In a photo of the *New York* taken off Rockaway on April 23, 1919, several features of interest are in view. On the rear of the main top is the aft range clock. On top of the king posts of the boat cranes are 3-inch/50-caliber antiaircraft gun mounts, surrounded by splinter mattresses. These mounts had been added sometime after December 1916. An aft torpedo-defense platform on the mainmast below the aft searchlight platform had been added after December 1916. Also, faintly visible on the sides of turrets 1, 2, and 4 are deflection scales, painted on to allow fire controllers in adjacent ships to know the azimuth of a target to be fired on. *National Archives*

This undated view of the *New York* from off its starboard stern probably was taken upon its return to New York from Europe in April 1919. On turret 4 is a deflection scale with tall scale marks, identical to the deflection scale seen in the preceding photo. The cover of the casemate at the stern was recessed slightly and could be opened. Within the next several years, this cover would be replaced by a permanent, unmovable cover. *National Archives*

USS *New York* is anchored in Hampton Roads, Virginia, in July 1919. Now, deflection scales were painted only on turrets 2 and 4, and the white numbers and scale now were white on a black band, for better visibility. The *New York* had been assigned to the Pacific Fleet and would soon depart for its new station at San Diego, California. *National Archives*

The battleship *New York* transits the Panama Canal in July 1919 en route to its new base in California. The ship was at this time heavily weathered and in need of new paint. A close inspection of this photo and others of the *New York* around this time suggests that the cage foremast had been painted black from the level of the tops of the smokestacks up to the bottom of the main top, and the cage mainmast had been painted black from top to bottom.
National Archives

In another aerial view of USS *New York* transiting the Panama Canal in July 1919, it can be seen that the roofs of the gunhouses had large hatches with covers that were hinged at the rear, shown here tilted in the open position. Littering the deck are large objects that appear to be packing crates.
National Archives

The *New York* is navigating the east chamber of the Pedro Miguel Locks of the Panama Canal in July 1919. Sometime between April 1919 and July 1919, the two forward 5-inch casemate guns on each side of the hull were removed. These mounts had proved nuisances because their compartments got wet when the ship was in rough seas. Eliminating the guns allowed for the improved sealing of the casemate covers. A round plug with four small holes in it covers the gunport in the forward casemate.

USS *New York* is at anchor off a populated shoreline, dressed fore and aft with flags and pennants in an undated photograph probably taken around 1919–20. The turrets have the white deflection scales on black backgrounds that dated to mid-1919, but the enclosed pilothouse and torpedo-defense platforms added around 1920 are not yet present. *National Archives*

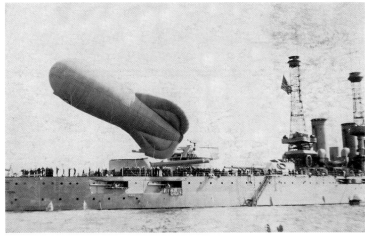

A barrage balloon, used for deterring attacking aircraft, is tethered to the starboard side of the quarterdeck of USS *New York* in an undated photograph taken most likely sometime between 1919 and 1920. The white deflection scales on black backgrounds on turrets 2 and 4 were introduced in mid-1919, and the open aft torpedo-defense platform seen here below the aft searchlight platform was replaced by an enclosed platform by January 1921.

The battleship *New York* departs from San Diego on January 7, 1921, bound for Grand Fleet maneuvers off the coast of South America. Two years later, the US Navy would begin a series of annual maneuvers known as fleet problems, large-scale training exercises that simulated possible war scenarios in the Pacific, the Caribbean, and the Atlantic. New features installed since the July 1919 photographs include a fully enclosed pilothouse and navigating bridge with a rangefinder on its roof, and a fully enclosed forward torpedo-defense platform immediately above the pilothouse. Also, the forward searchlight platform had been moved higher up the foremast. *National Archives*

On January 2, 1923, USS *New York* is anchored in San Diego Harbor, taking on supplies from several barges. Lying next to the battleship is the minesweeper USS *Brant* (AM-24). In addition to the rangefinder mounted atop the pilothouse, there now were similar rangefinders on the rear of the roofs of turrets 3 and 4. Also on each of those two turrets were two 3-inch/50-caliber antiaircraft guns. *National Archives*

The *New York* cruised via the Panama Canal to the Caribbean to participate in the 1924 fleet problems. It is seen here from the starboard side on February 20, 1924, off Isla Culebra, Puerto Rico, which at that time was a naval reservation. Awnings are rigged over the quarterdeck and the forecastle. Note the myriad signal flags flying from the yardarms on the foremast and the fully enclosed aft torpedo-defense platform, added within the past several years. *National Archives*

In October 1924, during its stint in the Atlantic, USS *New York* visited Hampton Roads, Virginia, where it is seen at anchor. The deflection scales were still present on the sides of the gunhouses of turrets 2 and 4. The 3-inch guns on the roof of turret 4 and on the platforms atop the boat cranes are at full elevation. Note how the rangefinder on the pilothouse roof jutted out slightly from the front edge of the roof. *National Archives*

An aerial photograph dated August 6, 1925, shows the *New York* in San Diego Harbor. What looks at first glance like sailors standing at a railing on top of the aft smokestack is actually a part of the 3-inch antiaircraft gun platform atop the port boat crane. On top of turrets 3 and 4 are numerous boxes: these were ready-service 3-inch ammunition boxes. The ventilation hatches on all turret roofs except turret 1 are open. *National Archives*

The *New York* lies off the Oregon coast, forested with evergreen trees, during the period between around 1921, when the ship received its fully enclosed pilothouse and torpedo-defense platforms, and 1926, when the ship was rebuilt with tripod masts. At several points along the hull, sailors on staging planks are scraping rust or touching up the paint. *National Archives*

In this undated photograph, USS *New York* displays some of the hallmarks of its design from around 1923 to 1926, such as the fully enclosed pilothouse and torpedo-defense platforms on both cage masts. Unlike its sister ship, USS *Texas*, which acquired the ability to launch scout planes in late 1918 with the installation of a fly-off platform on turret 2, USS *New York* would not have that ability until a catapult was installed on turret 3 during the ship's 1926–27 rebuilding. *National Archives*

The USS *New York* is anchored off the California coastline sometime between about 1920 and 1926. On the side of the bow are two closely spaced, taut chains; they were used for towing paravanes, for cutting submarine-mine cables. The chains ran from each side of the forecastle down to the "clump," a skeg on the bottom of the bow with a hole through it. Paravane tow cables attached to swivels were hauled down underwater as close to the clump as possible before the paravanes were launched.
National Park Service

CHAPTER 4
Reconstruction

From 1926 to 1927, USS *New York* was rebuilt at the Norfolk Navy Yard in Virginia. As seen in an April 10, 1927, photograph of the battleship in drydock at Norfolk, this process included the removal of its cage masts, smokestacks, and antiaircraft mounts on top of the boat cranes, along with other modifications. In addition, the original coal-fired boilers were replaced by oil-fired boilers. *Maritime Quest*

While the terms of the Versailles Treaty severely limited the ability of Germany to rearm following World War I, the victorious Allied powers sought to further diminish the chances of international conflict by limiting naval armament. Representatives of Britain, France, Italy, and Japan met their American colleagues for a naval conference in Washington, DC, beginning in November 1921. Following weeks of negotiations, on February 6, 1922, representatives of these nations signed the Washington Naval Limitations Treaty.

The treaty not only limited the number and size of battleships for the signatories but also stipulated how quickly old ships could be replaced, with the service life of a battleship set at twenty years. According to the terms of the treaty, the earliest that *New York* could be replaced was 1938. While limiting upgrades in main armament, the treaty did allow extant battleships to gain up to 3,000 tons each in countermeasures against the evolving threats of torpedoes, aerial bombs, and plunging gunfire.

The Washington Treaty curtailed the construction of most new capital ships. At the time of the signing, the United States had a number of such ships under construction, some quite advanced. Most of these were scrapped on the builder's ways, although USS *Washington* (BB-47), 75.9 percent complete, had already been launched and was fitting out. It ultimately would be sunk, less machinery, as a target by the combined firepower of *Texas* and *New York*. The boilers and machinery from *Washington*, along with those of the other canceled battleships and battle cruisers, were salvaged, together with considerable armor plate, for use in a program to modernize existent ships within treaty limitations.

New York and its sister ship, *Texas*, would each receive six new Bureau Express oil-fired boilers originally intended for new battleships. These boilers would replace the fourteen coal-fired boilers originally installed in each of the *New York*-class battleships.

In addition to burning laboriously handled coal, these ships were also deficient in side, deck, and underwater protection. To increase underwater protection, "blisters" were added to the outside of the hull amidships. The blisters increased the beam of the ships, but the hydrodynamic effect of their addition was to increase the efficiency of the hull form. The result of this was that despite the increase in the ships' weight and beam, there would be no penalty in speed.

New York entered Norfolk Navy Yard in 1926 for a two-year modernization program to include the features outlined above, including the conversion from coal-fired to oil-fired, using the new boilers from canceled ships. Whereas the original boilers were exhausted through twin funnels, the new arrangement required only a single funnel. Much of the space originally consumed by coal bunkers became fuel oil tanks, which was

During the 1926–27 rebuilding, *New York*'s cage masts were replaced by tripod masts. Here, the upper part of the foremast is being hoisted to the ship. On top of the mast are the forward fire-control stations, comprising the forward battle lookout station above the secondary-battery control station. Later, a small compartment will be placed atop this structure, containing the main-battery control station. *National Archives*

USS *New York* General Data (Rebuilt)	
Displacement	
normal	28,700 tons
design full load	30,000 tons
Dimensions	
Length overall	573′ ¾″
Waterline length	565′ 7¼″
Maximum beam	106′
Protection (changes)	
Armor	70 lb. STS + 70 lb. NS applied to earlier 20 lb. STS + 20 lb. STS over magazines between barbettes 2 and 5. 70 lb. STS + 70 lb. NS added to existing 28 lb. STS + 12 MS over engines. 70 lb. STS + 70 lb NS added to existing 12 lb. MS over midships boilers. 70 lb. NS added to existing 12 lb. MS armor deck aft of number 5 barbette. On the half deck 70 lb. STS + 70 lb. NS added from aft edge of number 2 barbette to forward limit of lower armor belt. 70 lb. STS added to turret tops.
Longitudinal torpedo protection	Width by the addition of 5′ 5″ bulges to each side
Machinery	
Boilers	Six Bureau Express type; 285-psi / 417-degree F operating temperature
Engines	As before
Maximum speed	19.72 knots
Endurance	10 knots: 815,000 nautical miles
Generators	Four 300 kw 120-volt DC turbogenerator sets
Propellers	As before
Rudder	As before
Fuel oil	2,810 tons, normal; 4,600 tons, emergency
Diesel oil	35 tons (for boats)

further augmented by additional tankage created in the new antitorpedo blisters. Those blisters, which added protection against torpedoes and near misses by bombs, greatly impaired the sea keeping of the ship, allowing the ship to roll significantly in less than calm seas.

The cage masts and most of the superstructure were stripped away, and a new superstructure was erected. Improved fire control systems were to be fitted, and the increased weight meant that a tripod foremast was used rather than a cage mast. Aft, a dwarf tripod mast supported searchlights and radio antennas. Less visible was the increased armor protecting vital areas of the ship. An aircraft catapult was installed atop turret 3.

Following reconstruction, *New York* operated variously off both the East and West Coasts and, in 1937, transported Adm. Hugh Rodman, acting as the personal representative of President Roosevelt, to England for the coronation of King George VI. Later that year it was fitted with eight 1.1-inch/75-caliber AA guns. The following year it became the first large US warship to be equipped with radar, when an experimental XAF radar set was installed. The system exceeded expectations, leading to many US warships being equipped with radar.

During September 1939, *New York* began to take part in the Neutrality Patrol, enforcing nonaggression on the part of warring nations for a distance of 200 miles off the coasts of North and South America. In July 1941, it escorted a convoy moving US troops to Iceland.

Newly rebuilt USS *New York* stands off Norfolk Navy Yard on October 10, 1927. The dual smokestacks had been replaced by a single one, to the immediate rear of which was the new midship fire-control tower, comprising a main-battery control station over a secondary-battery control station. A tripod mainmast was now between turrets 3 and 4. *National Archives*

In the rebuilding of the *New York*, an antitorpedo blister, which also acted as a fuel-oil storage reservoir to supply the new boilers, was installed on each side of the hull. The top of the starboard blister is visible halfway up the side of the hull, above the waterline. Jutting from the upper part of the hull amidships were sponsons, which made it possible to move six of the 5-inch/51-caliber guns, three per side, up to main-deck level. *National Archives*

The three sponson-mounted 5-inch/51-caliber guns on the starboard side are shown, along with their light-colored sponson covers. Now, all the 5-inch mounts on the second deck, or gun deck, on the forward half of the ship had been eliminated and the corresponding sponsons covered. There remained four 5-inch/51-caliber sponson guns on each side of the gun deck. A paravane, a hydrofoil device that could be towed alongside the ship to cut the cables of submarine mines, is stored on barbette 2. Details also are available for the pilothouse, the tripod foremast, and the forward fire-control stations. *National Archives*

Further details of the new arrangement of the USS *New York* are shown in a view off the starboard side on October 10, 1927, off the Norfolk Navy Yard. The relative locations of and distances between the foremast, the smokestack, the midship fire-control tower, and the mainmast are evident. Barely visible is another new, and quite significant, feature added during the rebuilding: on top of the gunhouse of turret 3, there now was a catapult for launching scout planes. Deflection scales no longer were on the gunhouses. *National Archives*

In another image from the series of the newly rebuilt USS *New York* off Norfolk Navy Yard on October 10, 1927, a rangefinder is still on top of turret 4, but the 3-inch antiaircraft guns have been removed from the roofs of turrets 3, 4, and 5. At the top of the tripod portion of the mainmast was a lookout platform with safety rails, below which was a searchlight platform on the roof of a compartment that served as a movie projection booth, for showing motion pictures on a screen set up on the quarterdeck. *National Archives*

As seen in a view of the *New York* from astern off Norfolk Navy Yard, the aft range clock had been relocated to the lower part of the rear of the movie projection booth. Light-colored covers called bloomers were fitted over the 14-inch gun barrels and fastened with clips to the frontal plate of the gunhouses. From this angle, the new antitorpedo blisters and their flat tops are highly visible. *National Archives*

The *New York* visited the northeastern US coast in February 1929 and is seen here during that month off a shoreline with residential buildings and evergreen trees. Although both the *New York* and its sister ship, the *Texas*, were rebuilt in the 1920s (*Texas* in 1925 and 1926) and were in many respects very similar after that rebuilding, their pilothouses were quite different in design. *Texas*'s pilothouse, built during World War I, had a noticeable bulge on the front and sides of the structure, below the windows. A feature added since late 1927 was the permanent windscreen at the front of the lookout platform on the mainmast.

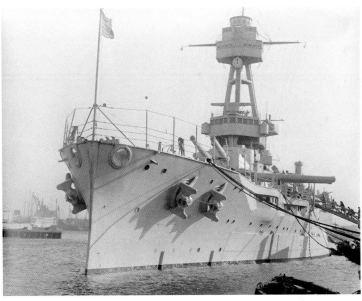

The *New York* is moored at a pier at the Boston Navy Yard on New Year's Day 1930. The covers over the casemates with the portholes seem to have been installed not during the 1926–27 rebuilding of the *New York*, but sometime between the photos of the ship transiting the Panama Canal in July 1919 and the January 1921 aerial photograph of the battleship.

The original inscription on this photo of the *New York* indicates that it was taken on September 18, 1929, at "Pier 5, Locust Point," which was located in Baltimore Harbor, Maryland. The battleship was part of a US Navy flotilla visiting Baltimore to commemorate the 200th anniversary of the city's chartering, and on September 12, sailors and Marines of the crew joined in a parade celebrating that anniversary.

USS *New York* is seen from farther away at a pier at Boston Navy Yard, New Year's Day 1930. The forward range clock was at the top of the foremast. A small platform with a windbreaker was on each side of the pilothouse. Of interest are the bloomers on turrets 1 and 2: they are of different designs, and those on turret 1 are of a dark color, while those on turret 2 are light colored.

This photo off USS *New York*'s starboard bow appears to have been taken at Boston Navy Yard: note the shed with the stovepipe to the far right in this photo and the preceding one. The 5-inch gun mount at the forward end of the superstructure deck has a fabric cover over it, with the gun barrel remaining exposed.

A photographer from Naval Air Station Coco Solo, on the Atlantic side of the Panama Canal, snapped this photo of USS *New York* on February 12, 1930. A rolled-up awning is stretched above the forecastle, and another awning is rigged alongside barbette 2. The bloomers on the turrets have been hitched up, exposing the lower halves of the 14-inch gunports. To the far right is what appears to be USS *Texas*. *National Archives*

Two letter *E*s representing battle-efficiency awards are on the smokestack of USS *New York* in an undated photo taken around 1932. The roof of turret 3 is painted a dark color with reference to the other four turret roofs. *National Archives*

An undated photograph shows the *New York* at sea sometime after its 1926–27 rebuilding. Machine gun tubs added to the foretop and the mainmast in 1933 or 1934 are not yet present. The forward range clock was located below the front of the foretop at a much-higher level than before the ship's rebuilding. *National Archives*

In a February 27, 1932, photo taken from an aircraft from USS *Saratoga*, the wing of which is in the foreground, the *New York* displays two *E*s on the smokestack, indicating that the ship's crew had won two battle-efficiency awards for that year. On the level of the superstructure where the pilothouse was before the *New York* was rebuilt, there now was the flag plot; the compartment, along with several of its portholes, is visible just aft of the conning tower. The battleship's number, 34, was now painted on the roof of turret 2 but is barely visible in this photo. *National Archives*

USS *New York* is viewed from the starboard side sometime between 1933 and 1936. A paravane is being hoisted along the hull abeam turret 1. A scout plane is on the catapult, and another one is on the quarterdeck adjacent to the mainmast. They appear to be Vought Corsairs, either O2Us or O3Us. *National Archives*

A battle line comprising, *front to rear*, USS *New York*, USS *Nevada* (BB-36) and USS *Oklahoma* (BB-37) passes by during fleet maneuvers in 1932. In the background, between *New York* and *Nevada*, is the carrier USS *Langley* (CV-1).

In this January 24, 1933, aerial photo of USS *New York*, a scout plane is perched on the catapult on top of turret 3. The aircraft is indistinct but appears to have been a Vought O2U Corsair. As many as three scout planes were carried on the *New York* at various times. Four guns are visible on the port side of the superstructure deck. From front to rear they are a 5-inch/51-caliber gun and three 3-inch/50-caliber antiaircraft guns (the rear one is adjacent to the boat crane). The 3-inch guns were mounted on this deck during the 1926–27 rebuilding. *National Archives*

This undated photograph of USS *New York* shows it after its 1926–27 rebuilding, with tripod masts present. The ship's number, 34, is painted in large numerals on the turret 2 roof, a feature that dates this photo to the period of approximately 1934 to 1938, when the practice of painting battleship numbers on turret roofs was current. *National Archives*

All 14-inch guns and the two aft 5-inch guns are trained to starboard on USS *New York* during maneuvers in Panama Bay, on the Pacific side of the Panama Canal, April 21, 1934. This was during Fleet Problem XV, and on this date the fleet was engaged in Exercise L, which entailed the concentration of forces off the Pacific entrance to the Panama Canal. Two noticeable changes had been made to the masts since the January 1933 photo: tubs for .50-caliber antiaircraft machine guns had been added to the front and the rear of the foretop, the upper part of the mainmast had been removed, and a new "birdbath" platform for four .50-caliber machine guns was installed on top of the mainmast. *National Archives*

USS *New York* is seen from astern in the foreground in this aerial photo of a column of battleships on May 31, 1934. That the crews of the battleships are lining the rails indicates that this was a special occasion: President Franklin D. Roosevelt's review of the fleet in the Atlantic off New York City. The wingtips of a scout plane on the catapult on turret three are visible. *National Archives*

USS *New York* is anchored off San Pedro, California, on April 18, 1935. From this angle, both of the .50-caliber antiaircraft machine gun tubs on the foretop are visible. At this time, battleships of the Battle Fleet, as the US Pacific fleet was then designated, had their ship number painted in white atop turret 2, with the tops of the numbers toward the front of the turret. The number "3" of the *New York*'s number, 34, is faintly visible on the roof of turret 2.

The *New York* cruises off the coast near San Diego, California, on August 23, 1935. During the 1926–27 rebuilding of the ship, the rangefinder on the roof of turret 4 had been moved from a position near the rear of the roof to one near the center of the roof, to the right side of the fore-aft centerline. *National Archives*

New York is seen from the starboard side in another August 1935 photograph. As was the practice in the interwar years, a full complement of boats and launches are stored onboard, including several that are nested one atop the other next to the king post of the boat crane. *National Archives*

A beautiful head-on view of USS *New York* shows the ship as configured in the mid-1930s. It shows the same arrangement of dark-colored bloomers on the 14-inch guns of turret 1, light-colored bloomers on the guns of turret 2, and what appears to be a canvas hood on the roof of turret 2, as seen in the preceding photo. *National Archives*

Although no date accompanied this photo of the *New York*, the presence of machine gun tubs on the foretop and the mainmast indicate it was taken after 1933 or 1934, and the absence of the antiaircraft fire-control station between the legs of the foremast on the antiaircraft control platform on top of the pilothouse indicates a date preceding June 1936, by which time that station had been constructed. Note the fuselage and tail of a scout plane stored on the aft part of the quarterdeck. *National Archives*

USS *New York* is docked at the Navy Yard, Puget Sound, in Bremerton, Washington, on June 1, 1936, undergoing periodic maintenance, repairs, and modernization. A new feature was the antiaircraft fire-control station, a structure with slanted panels with windows between the legs of the foremast on the antiaircraft control platform on top of the pilothouse.

This undated photograph of USS *New York* can be dated to 1934 or the several years following, judging from the presence of the machine gun tub on the front of foretop, installed by April 1934, and the type of aircraft that the port boat crane is hoisting aboard, a Vought O3U. *National Archives*

In a January 1937 photograph, the recently installed antiaircraft fire-control station on top of the pilothouse is visible. Sailors are on planks suspended along the hull, applying fresh paint—a never-ending task on any ship. Moored amidships is an officers' barge. Farther forward, a boarding ladder is rigged.

USS *New York* is at anchor in a May 1937 photo. The rear of the antiaircraft fire-control station between the aft legs of the foremast is visible from this angle: it had an inward-tilted upper panel with five windows. Immediately aft of the smokestack, the midship fire-control tower consists of, *from top to bottom*, main-battery control, secondary-battery control, a fruit locker, and a ventilator housing.

In a February 1938 photograph, USS *New York* rides at anchor off Culebra, Puerto Rico. A huge awning is rigged over the main deck from the forecastle to the front of the superstructure. A smaller awning is erected over much of the superstructure deck. The ship had been reassigned from the Pacific to the Atlantic the previous July. The ship's number, 34, was still present in white on the roof of turret 2. *National Archives*

On July 26, 1938, while steaming to Norfolk, Virginia, USS *New York* suffered a broken starboard propeller shaft. The ship proceeded to Norfolk Navy Yard on one engine and is shown in drydock there, undergoing repairs. Lines and chains were wrapped around the propeller and the shaft to secure them. A good view is available of the two aft starboard casemates.

The break in the starboard propeller shaft is shown close-up in a photo taken on August 12, 1938. On the right half of the photo is the stern tube bearing.

The starboard propeller, propeller shaft, and struts and the chains and lines securing them are viewed from a different angle. The propeller shaft had sheared off at the point where it entered the hull.

The fragments of the shattered propeller shaft are documented in this photo. The letters *A* through *D* were marked on several of the fractured surfaces to indicate where the parts fit together.

In 1938, the USS *New York* was selected as the test bed for the revolutionary new XAF radar. The "bedspring" antenna for the XAF radar was mounted at the former location of the rangefinder above the pilothouse; the rangefinder was moved to the roof of turret 2. Developed by the Naval Research Laboratory and installed in the *New York* in December 1938, the XAF operated at 200 megacycles, with a 1.5-meter wavelength and a power of 15 kilowatts.

The XAF bedspring antenna is viewed from the port side of the ship. The antenna could be rotated and tilted to better acquire aircraft. After the equipment was installed, the ship put the radar through its paces for the following three months during exercises in the Caribbean. The Brewster Aeronautical Corporation fabricated the antenna.

In 1940, the USS *New York* hosted the midshipmen of the United States Naval Academy on their traditional summer cruise. The battleship is shown at anchor off Annapolis, Maryland, on June 8, 1940. By then, the XAF bedspring antenna had been removed and the rangefinder remounted on top of the pilothouse. On the catapult are two Curtiss SOC scout planes. *National Archives*

USS *New York* is viewed from the starboard side toward the end of a two-month-long overhaul at the Norfolk Navy Yard on January 27, 1942. The ship had been repainted in a Measure 12 Graded System. This camouflage scheme consisted of Navy Blue on the hull with splotches of Ocean Gray toward the top; Ocean Gray with splotches of Haze Gray on the superstructure; and Deck Blue on horizontal surfaces. On the platform jutting from the rear of the foretop is a CXAM-1 radar antenna. The smaller antenna on the center of the roof of the foretop is a Mk. 3 parabolic fire-control radar antenna.

New York was in Norfolk Navy Yard for overhaul when the Japanese struck Pearl Harbor. With the world again at war, the Versailles Treaty limitations were no longer binding, so the main battery of *New York* was modified to allow an increase in elevation of up to 30 degrees, effectively increasing the range of its guns. This modification had been one that was long desired by the Navy but was forbidden by the treaty, which had limited improvements to main armament. With the attack on Pearl Harbor removing so many US battleships, at least temporarily, from operation, work on *New York* was accelerated and some repairs postponed in order to return it to operational status; it rejoined the fleet four weeks after the Japanese attack.

Initially, *New York* resumed its Atlantic patrols, as well as escorting convoys. A midyear refit brought about an increase in its antiaircraft armament, after which it again provided convoy escort. In October, it stood out from Norfolk, bound for Morocco and participation in Operation Torch, the Allied invasion of North Africa.

On November 8, during this action, *New York* was supporting the landings of the 47th Infantry Regiment when transports came under fire from enemy 130 mm guns at Point de la Tour. *New York* turned its 14-inch/45-caliber main guns on the enemy position and opened fire. One round ricocheted into a strongpoint, killing the battery commander and destroying the rangefinder. *New York* steamed toward Casablanca, Morocco, lest it need to deal with the enemy battleship *Jean Bart*, but that threat was neutralized by *Massachusetts*. *New York* retired from North Africa on November 14, having fired sixty main battery rounds during Operation Torch.

Thereafter, *New York* resumed convoy escort service until a refit in early 1943, which added even more antiaircraft weapons, raising it to ten 3-inch/50-caliber guns, forty 40 mm guns, and thirty-six 20 mm guns. At this time, it began to be used as a training ship, with 11,000 enlisted men and 750 officers being trained aboard between July 1943 and June 1944.

However, in late 1944, the decision was made to send *New York* back to the Pacific, and back into combat. Arriving in Long Beach on December 9, *New York* conducted refresher training off the California coast until January 12, when it steamed for Pearl Harbor. After refueling and taking on ammunition, it stood out for Ulithi to join several other older battleships to form a support force for the Iwo Jima landings. En route, one blade of its portside propeller was lost, reducing its maximum speed to 13 knots. This caused it to be detached from the task group and routed to Eniwetok to assess the damage and await orders. After two days at Eniwetok, it was decided to forgo repairs, and *New York* steamed to Saipan for rehearsals for the Iwo Jima assault. Handicapped by the damaged screw, *New York* left Saipan early for Iwo Jima, which it began shelling on February 16, at one point closing to within 1,000 yards of its target. *New York* shelled the island for three days, expending over 1,000 main battery rounds, more ammunition than any other ship present.

On the day of the Iwo Jima invasion (D-day), *New York* was ordered to Saipan, losing a blade from its starboard screw while en route and thereby limiting its speed to 4 knots.

New York is viewed from astern during the early-1942 refitting at Norfolk Navy Yard. The raised letters spelling "NEW YORK" on both sides of the stern were no longer picked out in contrasting colors. The ship's number was painted on both sides of the stern as well as the bow. The ship's antiaircraft battery had been significantly beefed up, as will be discussed. *National Archives*

In a view down and aft from the mainmast, the 14-inch guns of turret 4 are over the roof of the gunhouse of turret 5. The large ventilation hatches on the rear part of the roofs of the gunhouses as built had been eliminated and plated over. Life rafts are lashed to toe rails along the edges of the gunhouse roof. Flanking turret 5 are four newly mounted 20 mm antiaircraft guns, two to a side and fitted with covers, within splinter shields that also contain ready-service ammunition lockers. *National Archives*

As seen in a view off the port bow of the *New York* at Norfolk Navy Yard on January 27, 1942, the antiaircraft control platform on top of the pilothouse had been revamped, with a steel bulwark on its front. A tub for a 20 mm antiaircraft gun had been added to each front corner of the pilothouse. To the upper rear of the pilothouse there now were two tubs for 3-inch gun directors; the port one is visible. *National Archives*

Another photo from January 27, 1942, at Norfolk Navy Yard shows new gun mounts on the starboard side. The view is from the bridge looking aft. The first two guns are 3-inch/50-caliber, while to the rear is a quad 1.1-inch/75-caliber automatic gun mount. Both types of guns seen here were virtually obsolete by this time. Deflection scales in 10-degree increments are marked on the insides of the splinter shields for crew reference. *National Archives*

As seen from the forecastle, during the 1941–42 refitting, tubs for gun directors had been installed on the tops of the king posts of the boat cranes. Where the 5-inch guns used to be situated at the front of the superstructure deck, there were now platform extensions with splinter shields, behind which were extra 3-inch antiaircraft guns. *National Archives*

In a view of the aft fire-control tower facing forward from the top of the mainmast, a newly installed Mk. 3 fire-control radar antenna is on the roof of the midship main-battery control. The new tubs for gun directors atop the boat cranes are to the sides of the smokestack. Toward the top of the photo is the newly added CXAM-1 radar antenna, on a platform to the rear of the roof of forward main-battery control. In the background, new gun tubs are visible. *National Archives*

Replacement propellers were installed at Manus, and *New York* rejoined Task Force 54 at Ulithi on March 22 in preparation for the bombardment of Okinawa, which began on the twenty-seventh. *New York* was on station off Okinawa for seventy-six days, firing 4,159 rounds of 14-inch ammunition and 7,001 5-inch rounds. While off Okinawa it endured the only kamikaze attack it would be subjected to. Fortunately, the Japanese aircraft struck only one of *New York*'s Kingfisher observation planes, destroying it and injuring two men on deck.

Following this action, *New York* put into Pearl Harbor to have its worn-out 14-inch gun linings replaced in preparation for supporting the planned invasion of Japan.

While it was still at Pearl Harbor when the Japanese surrendered, *New York*'s service was far from over.

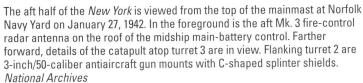

The aft half of the *New York* is viewed from the top of the mainmast at Norfolk Navy Yard on January 27, 1942. In the foreground is the aft Mk. 3 fire-control radar antenna on the roof of the midship main-battery control. Farther forward, details of the catapult atop turret 3 are in view. Flanking turret 2 are 3-inch/50-caliber antiaircraft gun mounts with C-shaped splinter shields. *National Archives*

The catapult and its launching car are in the foreground of this January 27, 1943, photo taken from atop turret 3, facing aft toward the mainmast. During this refitting, the number of 36-inch searchlights on the searchlight platform had been reduced from four to two, with a 20 mm antiaircraft gun replacing each of the removed searchlights. A curved splinter shield was installed around each 20 mm gun, but the two remaining searchlights still had railings around them. The framing on the underside of the birdbath machine-gun platform is visible. *National Archives*

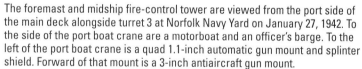

The foremast and midship fire-control tower are viewed from the port side of the main deck alongside turret 3 at Norfolk Navy Yard on January 27, 1942. To the side of the port boat crane are a motorboat and an officer's barge. To the left of the port boat crane is a quad 1.1-inch automatic gun mount and splinter shield. Forward of that mount is a 3-inch antiaircraft gun mount.

This January 27, 1942, photograph was taken on the port side of the stern, with turrets 4 and 5 in the foreground and the mainmast (sometimes referred to as the aftermast) and the port boat crane in the background. The two men on the roof of turret 4 are standing next to the open rear door of the rangefinder, which is traversed to point to the port side. Recently, tubs for sky lookouts had been installed on the aft corners of the searchlight platform. *National Archives*

Following its major refitting, USS *New York* stands off Norfolk Navy Yard on February 1, 1942, displaying its new Measure 12 Graded System camouflage from the starboard side. From this distance, some of the new additions are visible, such as the sky lookout tubs on the rear of the searchlight platform, the new radar antennas, and the splinter shields for the gun mounts on the superstructure deck. *National Archives*

An undated aerial photo captures a view of USS *New York* while painted in the Measure 12 Graded System scheme that it wore through the first half of 1942. Two Vought Kingfishers scout planes are visible on the catapult. Very dark-colored bloomers are present on the 14-inch guns. *National Archives*

USS *New York* and the escort carrier USS *Charger* (AVG-30, soon to be redesignated ACV-30) are docked side by side at the Norfolk Naval Yard, Portsmouth, Virginia, on August 11, 1942. During the refitting earlier that year, two 20 mm gun mounts and splinter shields had been added to the front of the *New York*'s pilothouse, and two 20 mm mounts and splinter shields were now on the level above the pilothouse, flanking the rangefinder. Two Vought OS2U-3 Kingfisher scout planes are mounted in tandem on the catapult. Note how the awning over the main deck fits around the roof of turret 1.

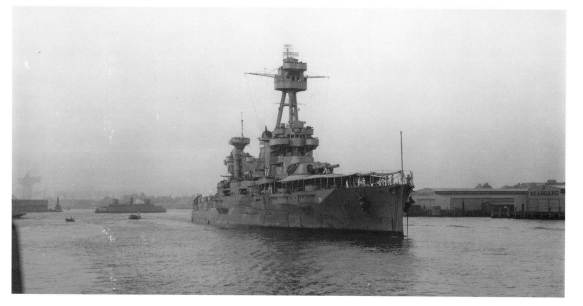

On August 12, 1942, USS *New York* is anchored in the Elizabeth River off the Norfolk Navy Yard. The awning is still rigged over the main deck; note how the portion of the awning over the forecastle is rolled up. Visible above the foretop are the big CXAM-1 radar antenna and, below it, the smaller Mk. 3 fire-control radar antenna. Early that year, the .50-caliber machine guns and gun tub on the front of the foretop had been replaced by 20 mm antiaircraft guns and a new design of tub. *National Archives*

The *New York* is observed off the starboard quarter on August 12, 1942. Note the wavy camouflage schemes on the 14-inch gun barrels. The rear of the antiaircraft fire-control station between the aft legs of the foremast, which previous to the 1941–42 refitting had five windows in it, now had a single window at the center. The prewar machine gun tub on the rear of the middle level of the foretop had been replaced in the refitting by a much-smaller tub made of welded plates. The stern casemate guns had been removed and their openings plated over. *National Archives*

In late 1942, USS *New York* participated in Operation Torch, the Allied invasion of North Africa. As part of the Southern Attack Group, it bombarded Safi Harbor in Morocco on November 8 and subsequently supported the Center Attack Group during the bombardment of Casablanca. The *New York* is seen here after the November 10 Battle of Casablanca. Sometime after mid-August 1942, the ship's Measure 12 Graded System had been painted over with Measure 22 Graded System, comprising Navy Blue (5-N) on the hull to a horizontal line at the lowest point of the main deck; Haze Gray (5-H) on vertical surfaces from that line upward; and Deck Blue (20-B) on horizontal surfaces. Three Vought Kingfishers are stored on the catapult. *National Archives*

While escorting a convoy across the Atlantic bound for Casablanca in March 1943, large waves crash over the deck of USS *New York*. Note the contrast between the Deck Blue paint on the turret roofs, the sills at the bottoms of the sides of the turrets, and the tops of the sight hoods, and the much-lighter Haze Gray on the vertical surfaces.

After returning from convoy escort duty to Casablanca, USS *New York* rests at the Navy Yard, New York, on April 27, 1943, undergoing some maintenance and refits. On the port side of the main deck is a temporary hut for workmen. Arrows and numbers indicate recently installed antennas on the yardarms of the foremast, including "stovepipe" identification, friend or foe (IFF) antennas.

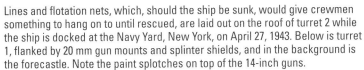

Lines and flotation nets, which, should the ship be sunk, would give crewmen something to hang on to until rescued, are laid out on the roof of turret 2 while the ship is docked at the Navy Yard, New York, on April 27, 1943. Below is turret 1, flanked by 20 mm gun mounts and splinter shields, and in the background is the forecastle. Note the paint splotches on top of the 14-inch guns.

In a view from the mainmast of USS *New York* facing forward at the Navy Yard, New York, on April 27, 1943, in the background are the midship fire-control tower and, farther forward, the foremast and foretop. On top of the boat crane king posts are tubs with Mk. 51 directors, for directing the antiaircraft guns. Mk. 51 directors also are in the tubs to the lower right and the lower left of the photo.

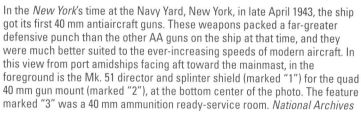

In the *New York*'s time at the Navy Yard, New York, in late April 1943, the ship got its first 40 mm antiaircraft guns. These weapons packed a far-greater defensive punch than the other AA guns on the ship at that time, and they were much better suited to the ever-increasing speeds of modern aircraft. In this view from port amidships facing aft toward the mainmast, in the foreground is the Mk. 51 director and splinter shield (marked "1") for the quad 40 mm gun mount (marked "2"), at the bottom center of the photo. The feature marked "3" was a 40 mm ammunition ready-service room. *National Archives*

Two quad 40 mm gun mounts were installed on the quarterdeck of the USS *New York* by the time this photo was taken on April 27, 1943. The view is from aft of the two mounts. The numbers "1" indicate the two splinter shields for the Mk. 51 directors associated with these 40 mm gun mounts. The numbers "2" to each side of the photo indicate the two quad 40 mm gun mounts. The number "3" indicates a waterproof bucket ventilator. *National Archives*

The USS *New York* is seen from the starboard side in an August 18, 1943, aerial photograph. At this time, the battleship was serving as a training ship in Chesapeake Bay. Specifically, from July 1943 to June 1944 the ship hosted a main-battery gunnery school and a destroyer-escort gunnery school.

USS *New York* appears in this undated photo painted in Measure 22 Graded System camouflage, the scheme in which the ship was painted between mid-August 1942 and the fall of 1944. The ship is rigged quite similarly to the appearance in the preceding photo and, though probably not taken on the same date, most likely was taken in or around August 1943 in Chesapeake Bay. Note the chains at the bow for rigging paravane tow cables. *National Archives*

In 1943, Pottsville Castings & Machine Shops of Pottsville, Pennsylvania, manufactured four new intermediate-pressure cylinders for USS *New York*'s engines at a cost of $20,500. Intermediate-pressure cylinders were part of a series of three pressure cylinders, ranging from high pressure to intermediate to low pressure, which had the successive effect of conditioning steam in the engine by expanding its volume while lowering its pressure. This intermediate-pressure cylinder was photographed at Norfolk Navy Yard on September 25, 1943. *National Archives*

The training compartment for the Mk. 51 director is viewed from another angle, with the movie projector to the left, the trainee on the training version of the Mk. 51 director to the right, and a movie screen in the background. The gun director's job required great skill and judgment and lightning-fast reflexes, so adequate training was a must. *National Archives*

This June 3, 1944, photograph shows a compartment in USS *New York* for instructing gun directors how to use a training version of the Mk. 51 director. This director (*left*) was used to remotely control a quad 40 mm gun mount, and it comprised a Mk. 14 computing gunsight on a pedestal mount, with handlebars to control the traverse and elevation of the sight, and shoulder rests. To the rear, a trainer runs a film projector; the director-trainee will track the projected image through the computing sight. *National Archives*

During the *New York*'s stint as a gunnery training ship, some of its 20 mm antiaircraft guns were equipped with training sights, as shown here. The gunner was strapped to the gun carriage, with his shoulders cradled in shoulder rests; he aimed the gun and elevated it largely by shifting his body around. On the pedestal mount is a handwheel for raising and lowering the gun carriage, in order to aid the gunner in achieving the desired elevation of the gun. Note the azimuth marks on the splinter shield. *National Archives*

The training sight for the 20 mm gun is viewed from the right side. It seems to have incorporated some type of movie-viewing device; on the lower rear of the side of the device was a sprocket, around which was an endless chain that was attached to a device on the trunnion. *National Archives*

In late 1944, USS *New York* was assigned to the Pacific Fleet. It is shown at Norfolk Navy Yard, Virginia, on November 14, 1944, before departing for the Pacific. The ship had been repainted in Measure 31a Design 8B camouflage, which incorporated patterns of Haze Gray (5-H), Ocean Gray (5-O), and Navy Blue (5-N) on vertical surfaces and Deck Blue (20-B) on horizontal surfaces. *National Archives*

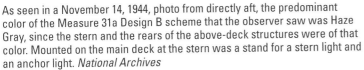

As seen in a November 14, 1944, photo from directly aft, the predominant color of the Measure 31a Design B scheme that the observer saw was Haze Gray, since the stern and the rears of the above-deck structures were of that color. Mounted on the main deck at the stern was a stand for a stern light and an anchor light. *National Archives*

USS *New York* is viewed from dead ahead at Norfolk Navy Yard on November 14, 1944. The radar-antenna array above the foretop had been revamped. Months earlier, before June 1944, the CXAM-1 bedspring antenna had been replaced. In addition, two new Mk. 50 directors for controlling the 3-inch and 40 mm antiaircraft batteries were installed on the ship, including one at the front of the pilothouse roof, replacing the rangefinder. *National Archives*

The new Mk. 50 director on the pilothouse roof is seen more clearly in this photo from November 14, 1944.
The front of the platform the director was mounted on had a new, steel bulwark. The Mk. 50 director
featured a Mk. 10 Mod. 5 scanning radar with a 45-inch dish-type antenna.

The *New York* was photographed off the starboard beam at an altitude of 200 feet on November 14, 1944. In view is a recently installed small platform with a steel bulwark on the front leg of the mainmast. The structures on top of the mainmast also had been radically reworked.

The patterns of the new camouflage scheme and the structural changes on top of the mainmast following the fall 1944 modernization of USS *New York* are seen from a different angle in another photo from November 14, 1944. There now were four levels of platforms and compartments on the mainmast, with the searchlight platform now on the bottom level and the aft Mk. 50 director above the top level.

A tugboat and two smaller craft accompany the *New York* in Hampton Roads, Virginia, on November 14, 1944. On the 14-inch gun barrels of turrets 1 and 2, the color demarcation between the Haze Gray to the fronts and the darker Ocean Gray to the rears is visible. Not apparent in this photo is the fact that the instructions for the *New York*'s Measure 31a Design B scheme called for painting the inside half of each mast leg Ocean Gray and the outside half Haze Gray.

USS *New York* is seen from astern in a final aerial photo from Hampton Roads on November 14, 1944. The upgrades recently made to the ship, particularly its antiaircraft fire-control system, would better prepare it for the intense battle environment of the Pacific theater.

USS *New York* is docked along the near side of the nearest pier, with a transport ship moored aft of it. The scene is the US Naval Dry Docks, Roosevelt Base, on Terminal Island, Long Beach, California, in December 1944. On the opposite side of the pier from USS *New York* is the USS *Arkansas* (BB-33), a *Wyoming*-class battleship.

The facilities at Roosevelt Base, Terminal Island, are viewed from the opposite direction of the preceding view, with USS *New York* docked in the background. The name of this facility was changed to Terminal Island Naval Shipyard on November 30, 1945.

The *New York* cruises off a coastline around late 1944 or early 1945. The Measure 31a Design B paint has weathered significantly since the November 14, 1944, photographs at Hampton Roads, suggesting that the ship was in the Pacific when this photo was taken.

Judging from the condition of the paint, this photo of USS *New York* probably was taken around the same time as the preceding one. At the time the structures on the mainmast were revised in the fall of 1944, an upper extension of the mainmast was installed on the front of those structures. It was fitted with two platforms with safety rails and a number of antennas.

In February 1945, USS *New York* participated in the pre-invasion shelling of Iwo Jima in support of US Marine Corps amphibious landings on that volcanic island. In a view from amidships facing aft, turret 4 is traversed to starboard, and its left 14-inch/45-caliber gun has just fired a round at a Japanese position on Iwo Jima on February 16, 1945, three days before D-day. *National Archives*

The big guns of the *New York* pound Japanese positions on Iwo Jima. The view is from aft of the port rear leg of the foremast facing forward. On the lower platform to the right is an antiaircraft gun director. *National Archives*

The flag-draped bodies of three US Navy personnel who had died of their wounds and had been brought aboard USS *New York* during operations off Iwo Jima in February 1945 are being prepared for burial at sea. At the center, Navy chaplain D. S. Rankin performs the committal service while the band, attendants, and members of the crew stand by. *National Archives*

Sailors on the *New York* hoist aboard a wounded man on a stretcher during operations off Iwo Jima. To the left is a gallery of 20 mm antiaircraft guns and a mooring bitt. *National Archives*

The remains of one of the USN casualties at Iwo Jima is being committed to the deep. Although the three men who were committed to the sea from USS *New York* were not members of that ship's crew, the *New York*'s crew accorded them full honors of an at-sea military burial.

Following its return from the Pacific after the end of World War II, USS *New York* visits New York Harbor in order to participate in that city's gala Navy Day observances on October 27, 1945. During the week of the observances, US Navy warships were lined up on the Hudson River for seven miles. *National Archives*

The *New York* is seen from another perspective at the time of its October 27, 1945 visit to New York City. A Vought Kingfisher scout plane is mounted on the catapult. Among the dignitaries and VIPs who attended the Navy Day festivities in New York that year was President Harry S. Truman. *National Archives*

At the time of its visit to New York City for Navy Day 1945, USS *New York* had a war-weary appearance, with heavily weathered paint and much evidence of corrosion on the hull. However, the ship's name stood out in bright, white letters on the stern. *National Archives*

Sailors hail USS *New York* around the time of the 1945 Navy Day festivities. Affixed to the bulwark above the pilothouse is what appears to have been signs or scoreboards. There was a bittersweet tone to *New York*'s appearance at Navy Day, since the ship was scheduled for retirement.

The flotilla of US Navy warships on the Hudson River for Navy Day 1945 is viewed from the George Washington Bridge, with USS *New York* in the middle background, below the hovering blimp. This naval spectacle was a fitting celebration for New Yorkers of the recent victory in World War II.

Tugboats nudge USS *New York* toward Pier 51 in Manhattan on October 19, 1945, the week before Navy Day. The old battleship was celebrated in the New York press for its construction in that city and its participation in two world wars.

USS *New York* is docked at Pier 51 in Manhattan during its October 1945 visit to that city. Sometime in the final months of World War II, the Measure 31a Design 8B camouflage applied in the fall of 1944 was painted over, most likely in Measure 21 camouflage, with Navy Blue on vertical surfaces and Deck Blue on horizontal ones.

CHAPTER 6
The Atomic Age

The veteran battleship's next assignment was taking part in Operation Magic Carpet, the transport back home of thousands of soldiers. It sailed from Pearl Harbor on September 3, 1945, with 875 weary soldiers in addition to its crew, arriving in San Pedro (Los Angeles) on September 9 and discharging its passengers. It took aboard 880 servicemen and sailed again for Hawaii, where those men would relieve troops more senior, and thus eligible for discharge. Taking on 1,103 veteran servicemen, it left Pearl Harbor, transited the Panama Canal, and put into New York City on October 19 to participate in the Navy Day celebration there.

Following those celebrations, *New York* put into the Philadelphia Naval Shipyard, where it was prepared for use as a target in the atom bomb tests at Bikini Atoll.

New York left Philadelphia on March 4, 1946, destined for a stop at Pearl Harbor, after which it would proceed to Bikini, becoming one of seventy targets. However, while en route the tests were postponed, so *New York* put into San Francisco until May 1, which it again left for Pearl to have instruments and test gear placed aboard. *New York* at last arrived in Bikini Atoll on June 15, 1946, prepared to meet its fate.

On July 1, 1946, Test Able (Test A) was undertaken, with a B-29 dropping an atomic bomb at the orange-painted USS *Nevada*, at the center of the test fleet, with *New York* anchored 975 yards away at Berth 188. The bomber crew missed their target, with the result being that the *New York* was 1,555 yards away from the burst. *New York* survived the air blast of Test Able with remarkably little damage. Even more remarkable was that the bulk of *New York*'s crew reboarded it the same day as the test, and by July 2 the entire crew was back aboard!

Inspection by the crew found that the Mk III fire control radar was damaged and two small fires were started, and, not surprisingly, the side of the ship facing the blast (starboard) suffered paint scorching. The post–bomb inspection noted, "Vessel suffered only superficial damage" and "There was no flooding due to bomb detonation." However, the #2 fireroom was damaged by blast pressure coming down the stack. It was estimated that under normal circumstances the ship's crew would be able to repair this damage in three or four days. The Test Able report further stated that beyond the bulging of the boilers, "There is no other damage to machinery, of which has been operated since Test A."

Test Baker (Test B) was conducted on July 25, 1946. This test was the world's first underwater explosion of a nuclear device. The bomb, nicknamed "Helen of Bikini," was suspended 90 feet beneath LSM-60 and detonated there. No trace of the landing ship was subsequently found.

On July 28, a party of twenty-one men came aboard for an initial inspection and found that this blast opened several seams in *New York*'s aft trim tanks, permitting flooding of the starboard shaft alley, electric steering gear room, and aft diesel room. It was believed that had the ship been manned, this flooding could have quickly been controlled. There was considerable shock damage throughout the ship, with the inspection even noting that the shock lifted 14-inch shells out of stowage. Incredibly, these twenty-one men stayed aboard the radioactive ship for three days.

Despite the leaks and considerably more damage than had been wrought by the air blast, *New York* remained not only afloat but largely operable following the second atomic blast. On August 5, it was reported that due to radiation, personnel could be on the weather decks for three-quarters of an hour and below decks in most areas for eight hours, but the "*New York* is not habitable at this time." However, on August 7, scores of men worked aboard *New York* in two-hour increments in an effort to decontaminate the battleship: "The day was spent jettisoning useless, highly radioactive materials, particularly debris and wood items." These efforts continued for the next two days, paused, and then resumed from August 17 to 21. On August 22, *New York* began the two-day tow to Kwajalein Lagoon, where it was decommissioned on August 29. It lingered, rusting, subject to occasional inspection, until 1947, when incredibly it was towed to the Navy Yard at Pearl Harbor, arriving on March 15, and tied up in the shipyard. A study at the time confirmed that the ship was so contaminated with radiation that not even linens could be removed from the ship. Thus, on July 6, 1948, *New York* was towed forty miles out to sea and used as a target for nonnuclear weapons. On July 7, following an eight-hour barrage, it capsized and sank, serving the nation to the very end.

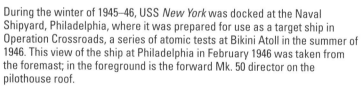

During the winter of 1945–46, USS New York was docked at the Naval Shipyard, Philadelphia, where it was prepared for use as a target ship in Operation Crossroads, a series of atomic tests at Bikini Atoll in the summer of 1946. This view of the ship at Philadelphia in February 1946 was taken from the foremast; in the foreground is the forward Mk. 50 director on the pilothouse roof.

A view from a similar perspective as in the preceding photo shows more of the starboard side of the main deck, along with the rear of the Mk. 50 director and details of the antiaircraft control platform the director is mounted on.

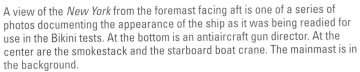

A view of the *New York* from the foremast facing aft is one of a series of photos documenting the appearance of the ship as it was being readied for use in the Bikini tests. At the bottom is an antiaircraft gun director. At the center are the smokestack and the starboard boat crane. The mainmast is in the background.

The *New York* is seen facing aft from the foremast at Philadelphia in February 1946. Many of the antiaircraft gun mounts and directors have been removed. Two Curtiss SC-1 scout planes are visible on deck.

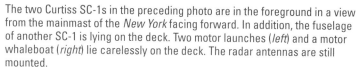

The two Curtiss SC-1s in the preceding photo are in the foreground in a view from the mainmast of the *New York* facing forward. In addition, the fuselage of another SC-1 is lying on the deck. Two motor launches (*left*) and a motor whaleboat (*right*) lie carelessly on the deck. The radar antennas are still mounted.

The three SC-1s on the USS *New York* are the focus of this February 1946 photo at the Naval Shipyard, Philadelphia. The light-colored shapes on the port side of the deck represent places where 20 mm antiaircraft gun pedestals had been removed.

The *New York*'s quarterdeck is viewed from one of the platforms on the mainmast in February 1946. Although the 20 mm antiaircraft guns and their splinter shields and the quad 40 mm antiaircraft guns had been removed from the deck, the semicircular splinter shields for the 40 mm guns remained in place, and a twin 40 mm gun mount and its director were now present on the starboard stern.

Tugboats assist the *New York* from its berth at the Naval Shipyard, Philadelphia, on March 4, 1946. The press referred to the ship as part of the "guinea-pig task force" that was bound for Bikini Atoll. The cover plates that had been installed over the stern casemates in the summer of 1942 are seen to good advantage.

USS *New York* lies off the Naval Shipyard, Philadelphia, on March 4, 1946, on the day of its departure on its final voyage, one that would end at Bikini Atoll. The dual 40 mm gun mount on the starboard side of the stern is visible. A Curtiss SC-1 fuselage lies next to turret 4.

The *New York* stopped at San Francisco on its last voyage. Its decks and platforms are eerily bereft of the scores of sailors that populated them during the ship's active service. Although most of the ship's 20 mm and 40 mm gun batteries had been removed, the main-battery guns as well as the 3-inch and 5-inch guns remained. *National Park Service*

The battleship *New York* passes under the Golden Gate Bridge as it departs from San Francisco on May 1, 1946, en route to Bikini Atoll. Two Curtiss SC-1 scout planes were still on the catapult on turret 3 at this point. *National Park Service*

USS *New York* is viewed from the starboard side not long before the Bikini atomic tests, the first of which was carried out on July 11, 1946. The ship's name had been painted in large letters on the starboard side of the hull to the side of turret 3. A Vought Kingfisher scout plane was mounted on the catapult. *Library of Congress*

The USS *New York* departs from San Francisco Bay on May 1, 1946. The decorations that appear to have been scoreboards or signs on the bulwark above the pilothouse, present in the photos of the ship at New York on Navy Day 1945, are still present.

On June 29, 1946, the skeleton crew of the USS *New York* gathers on the deck of the battleship and prepares to evacuate it, days before the first atomic test at Bikini. Their baggage is loaded on a cargo net for hoisting into the craft that will transport them away from the condemned ship. *National Archives*

The *New York* survived both atomic bomb tests at Bikini Atoll: Test Able, an air burst, on July 1, 1946, and Test Baker, a submerged burst, on July 25. For Test Able, the *New York* was a mere 1,545 yards from the epicenter of the bomb. Suffering only moderate damage from the blasts, the *New York* was decommissioned at Kwajalein on August 29, 1946, and later was towed by sea tugs from the test site to Pearl Harbor for further analysis of the effects of the blast on the ship. It is shown entering the harbor on March 19, 1947. *National Archives*

Five crewmen of USS *New York* dog-down a hatch before evacuating the ship during Operation Crossroads on June 29, 1946. They are, *from left to right*, K. R. Brook, S. P. Friedman, S. Welch, and R. Gross. *National Archives*

Eagle Scouts and naval personnel in a motor launch survey the *New York* during a tour of Pearl Harbor. In the background is the battleship *Nevada*, which also had been a target ship at the Bikini atomic tests and was slated for destruction as a target ship. *National Archives*

The two decommissioned battleships, *New York* (*left*) and *Nevada*, lie at anchor at Pearl Harbor on June 8, 1948, awaiting their fates as target ships. Although the *New York* had been on the East Coast at the time of the December 7, 1941, Japanese attack on Pearl Harbor, the *Nevada* had endured the attack, its crew putting up a heroic defense. *National Archives*

The rescue-and-salvage ship USS *Conserver* (ARS-39), out of the photo to the left, tows the battleship *New York* from Pearl Harbor on July 6, 1948. The large numbers and scales on the bow were applied to the ship at Pearl Harbor and apparently were reference markings with which to visually gauge the progress of the ship's settling and sinking. *National Archives*

At a point some forty miles southwest of Pearl Harbor on July 7, 1948, an aerial photographer captured this view of the *New York* two hours after the commencement of the bombardment of the old battleship. Among the ordnance the Navy planned to direct at the ship by aircraft of Task Force 38 were ASM-N-2 "Bat" bombs: radar-assisted, guided glide bombs. *National Archives*

The *New York* severely heels to port four hours after the commencement of the bombardment of the battleship on July 7, 1948. Thus far, the ship had absorbed hits from bombs no bigger than 500-pounders and shells no larger than 5-inch, but, despite plans to bombard the ship for two days, it would soon capsize. *National Archives*

The *New York* is smoking severely, and water is cascading from ruptures along the top of the starboard hull blister, in its final moments before capsizing. *National Archives*

The *New York* has turned turtle on July 7, 1948, and soon will sink. Despite the ignominious nature of this photo, it provides an extremely rare photographic view of the entire bottom of the hull of a US battleship. The forefoot, where the bottom of the bow transitions into the keel, is to the far left. Jutting from the forefoot is the clump, a type of skeg through which chains for a paravane-towing gear were passed. To the right is the rudder, and the various docking keels, and the contours of the starboard hull blister are visible. *National Archives*